S0-ANO-310

R01096 03660

HOW TO SAVE OUR SCHOOLS AND OUR NATION

by: **RODDY SCHNITZ**
AND
KELLY COLE

published by: Century Enterprises
1 Towers Park Lane
Suite 1006C
San Antonio, Texas 78209-6412
1-800-647-9978
(210) 829-4486
Fax: (210) 822-1031

AS
OUR
SCHOOLS
GO

SOCIAL SCIENCES DIVISION
CHICAGO PUBLIC LIBRARY
400 SOUTH STATE STREET
CHICAGO, IL 60605

SO
GOES
OUR
NATION

Printed in the USA by

MoRRIS
PUBLISHING

**3212 E. Hwy 30
Kearney, NE 68847
800-650-7888**

R01096 03660

This book is dedicated to the brave souls who go forth each day and face the perils of teaching our children in some of our schools.

SOCIAL SCIENCES DIVISION
CHICAGO PUBLIC LIBRARY
400 SOUTH STATE STREET
CHICAGO, IL 60605

BOOK...
...LIBRARY
...SOUTH...
...COLORADO

RESERVED

HOW TO SAVE OUR SCHOOLS AND OUR NATION

All rights reserved. Printed in the United States Of America. No part of this book may be used or reproduced in any form or by any means, or stored in a data base or retrieval system without prior written permission of the publisher except in the case of brief quotations embodied in critical articles and reviews. Making copies of this book for any purpose other than your own personal use is a violation of United States copyright laws.

The purpose of this book is to point out the deficiencies in our education system and to offer changes which could correct these deficiencies. In so doing, some may feel that they are being attacked personally. This is not the case, and the authors are to be held harmless, if any persons of any race, creed, color, or position feel that they are being singled out for criticism. The authors hope the contents of this book will be taken as it is offered which is for one purpose only, and that is to help to improve our education system.

The publisher offers a money back guarantee to anyone who reads this book, and is not satisfied with it for any reason.

Copyright 1995 by Roddy Schnitz
Library of Congress Catalog No. 95-69783
ISBN 0-9644775-0-5

CONTENTS

FOREWORD

AFTER READING THE TITLE, ONE COULD ASK:

"WHY DO OUR SCHOOLS AND OUR NATION NEED TO BE SAVED?"

THE ANSWER IS THEY ARE BOTH IN DEEP TROUBLE. WHY ARE THEY IN TROUBLE? SCHOOLS ARE IN TROUBLE, BECAUSE THEY ARE NOT EDUCATING ALL OF THEIR STUDENTS, AND THEIR GRADUATES ARE NOT QUALIFIED FOR THE ENTRY LEVEL JOBS IN THIS NEW AND HIGHLY TECHNICAL JOB MARKET. OUR COUNTRY IS IN TROUBLE BECAUSE THE SHORTAGE OF QUALIFIED WORKERS PREVENTS INDUSTRY FROM BEING ABLE TO COMPETE WITH OTHER NATIONS WHICH HAVE A HIGHLY TRAINED WORK FORCE. ANY NATION WHICH CANNOT COMPETE IN THIS NEW WORLD OF TECHNOLOGY AND TRADE WILL BECOME A THIRD RATE NATION. OUR COUNTRY IS HEADED IN THAT DIRECTION, AND THE ONLY THING WHICH WILL REVERSE THIS TREND IS A COMPLETE OVERHAUL OF OUR SCHOOL SYSTEM. IT'S LATER THAN YOU THINK, SO LET'S GET STARTED NOW.

PREFACE

In the course of our history, we have had numerous wars and battles. We have won all of them except one, Vietnam. All of the wars which we won were supported by the people. The United States is a great nation, and we can win any future war, if the war is supported by the people. Vietnam taught us this lesson.

In the 1930's, we had only one enemy - the great depression. We knew who the enemy was and selected a leader who promised to get us out of that terrible nightmare. It was more than a nightmare, it was real. We followed the leader, and all of us worked toward defeating hunger, poverty, and unemployment. We were united in our effort to defeat the enemy, and we did.

As we began to emerge from unemployment and hunger, a new enemy appeared on the scene. Hitler began rattling his sabre. We weren't sure he was our enemy until December 7, 1941, when the Japanese attacked Pearl Harbor. With this event there was a great awakening. We awoke with a resolve to destroy the enemy, and we became united in this effort. We knew who the enemy was, and what we had to do to defeat him. After a long and costly war we were victorious. We had to make sacrifices, but we were willing to do this because we knew we must defeat Germany and Japan.

About the time we began to enjoy peace in the

world, another enemy appeared on the scene - the Soviet Union. One of its leaders pounded his shoe on a table and promised to bury us and our capitalistic system. Even before this outburst, we had begun to recognize that the Soviet Union was a greater threat to our nation than Hitler was, because the Soviets had atomic bombs aimed at our cities and our defenses. This united us, and we began to arm ourselves "to the teeth."

Again, we were united in our effort because we knew who the enemy was, and knew what we had to do to win the war. As a result, we started on an arms race such as had never been done before. We built enough atomic bombs to almost blow the world off it's axis. Along with the bombs, we built airplanes, submarines, missile sites, cannons, and rockets with which to launch the bombs. Also, we started to build a 600 ship Navy. All of the arms build-up cost us more than we could afford. The debt became so great that at the end of the arms race, the national debt was greater than the combined debts at the end of each presidency since George Washington.

How did we create such a huge debt? The debt got out of hand for two reasons; one, we bought an over-kill number of weapons; and two, we bought them on credit. We lowered the income tax, thereby lowering the income of the nation, and we started an arms spending spree on credit. We will not address the debt in this book, because the authors do not have a solution, and neither does anyone else. The debt is an enemy many of us have not recognized. We now have an enemy we can't defeat, but

V

we must keep the debt in mind, because our debt is an enemy which affects how much we can spend on education.

The arms build-up did nothing more than to hold the enemy at bay. Thank goodness for that! The enemy's economic system defeated him. He went bankrupt, and we would have also gone bankrupt, if the arms race had continued much longer. The arms race left us being the greatest debtor nation in the industrialized world.

Now that the Soviet Union has defeated itself, many of us again relaxed and thought we did not have any more enemies. We were wrong. We now have an enemy who is already on our shores, and who is more deadly than an atomic bomb. That enemy is our defunct school system. Today our high school graduates are less educated than high school graduates in the early 1960's. This is the first time in history when children are less educated than their parents. It should have been the other way around, because knowledge doubles about every twelve years. Our schools should have prepared for and taught to higher levels. Our schools not only did not teach to higher levels, they have not taught to early 1960 levels. This is evidenced by the fact that Scholastic Achievement Test (SAT) scores have dropped about 70 points since 1963, and teachers give the same ratio of A, B, C, and D grades that they have always given. This tells us that we are letting the students set the standard. This is the worst possible mistake any training organization can make, but our school systems have made this mistake. Our so called educators have failed us. They have not only failed us, they have become part of the problem, because they do not know how to get the schools back to the pre-1963 level, and are not willing to ask for help.

We have lowered our education standard to the point where we are near the bottom when we compare our top students with top students from other countries. Also, most state colleges have remedial courses, and as many as 50% of their freshman and sophomore students are enrolled in these courses. Colleges also have watered-down college courses. Many of our high school graduates cannot read at the eighth grade level, and are illiterate in math and science.

The failure of our education system is now the enemy which we must do something. It is a self-inflicted enemy - an enemy we must defeat, or our country will go down the tube. Why will it go down the tube? It will because we will not be able to compete in this new technical/trade world, if we do not educate everyone. Any country which does not have a highly educated work force will not be able to survive as a first rate country.

Even though we have an enemy more deadly than an atomic bomb, many of us have not recognized this fact. The purpose of this book is to raise a red flag. In this book the problems will be defined and solutions will be offered. The solutions which will be offered won't be the band-aid solutions which are sometimes offered by educators and politicians.

Some of them will require drastic actions - the kinds of actions which will be necessary to defeat the enemy.

We can't defeat this enemy, if we don't all recognize that we have an enemy, and do whatever is necessary to win the education war. The authors hope that each reader will join the fight, and will rally the troops around the good old red, white, and blue as we have done in past wars. We must defeat this new, and not fully recognized, enemy.

INTRODUCTION

At the beginning of this century 90% of our population were farmers who needed only a grammar school education. As the years went by, more knowledge became available. Now the average job which pays a living wage requires at least two years of education beyond high school. In the future even more education will be required, because knowledge which is available to us doubles about every twelve years.

At the same time that more knowledge began to become available, our education system began to fail. We still have the best farmers in the world as evidenced by our being the world's largest food producer. However, in other jobs and professions, except medicine and the arms industry, we have fallen behind countries which we once considered to be "backward". We even included Japan in this category at one time.

How did we get so far behind? It happened because we did not increase our education level as more knowledge became available. In fact, since 1963 we have not been able to get our students to learn as much as students learned prior to 1963. Many of our high school graduates cannot read, write, and do math at the eighth grade level. This must change, and the changes which are necessary will be addressed in this book.

Before we go any further, let's examine the

causes. Unless we understand what caused the problem, we can't find solutions. The causes follow:

1. The deterioration of the family.
2. The decline of moral values in our society.
3. Our addiction to drugs, alcohol, television, and firearms.
4. The poor getting poorer (there is a direct relationship between poverty level and education level).
5. School administrators not being selected based on their ability to control and motivate students. Instead, they are being selected based on courses they have taken.
6. Watered-down laws which do not demand justifiable punishment for crimes committed, including crimes committed by juveniles.
8. The failure of the family to motivate, and discipline their children, and to become involved in the education of their children.
9. Our insatiable desire for material possessions.
10. Last, but not least, the Supreme Court's ruling which eliminated prayer in our schools.

These are the root causes, and fifty changes which must be made will be offered in Chapter II "How Bad?". How to make the changes will be offered in other chapters.

The authors have used "we" throughout this book because it is we who must take action to solve the school problems. "We" is defined as readers of this book and anyone we can enlist in the war for better education. Politicians and educators have not been able to solve the problems. Many of them have been found to be incompetent, and some of them have been found to be a part of the problem. Now, the average tax payer must take the bull by the horns and begin the long trek down the rough road to education reform.

So, as you read, be thinking about how you can make a difference. You can't do it alone, so get all the help you can. Go before your School Boards and talk change and ask for their help. Speak before PTA groups. Appear before your City Council, and ask that they become involved, and that they take action to cause the citizens to become involved. Enlist the help of teacher labor unions. Write letters to your State Education Agency. Call and write to your Governor and other politicians. Keep the pot boiling and stirred.

It's later than you think. Let's start by making changes now. We can't waste any more time, so read on and start moving and shaking.

CHAPTER I

WHY WE MUST EDUCATE EVERYONE

The "Why" is revealed on the chart on the next page. As the chart shows, we have changed from an agrarian society at the beginning of this century to a highly specialized and technical society today. In today's workplace there is not a need for the uneducated. Most manual labor jobs are done by machines which have been designed by the educated. There will not be many jobs for unskilled and uneducated workers in the future. There will be a few in food service, janitorial, and other fields where a great deal of skill is not required. However, there are not enough of these jobs to take care of our uneducated at the present time. There will be fewer manual labor jobs in the future, and the number of uneducated will increase dramatically in the next fifty years. There will be more on the increase in uneducated and unskilled in Chapter XI "Minorities and Athletics."

What must we do to solve this problem? We must educate all students to their fullest potential. How do we do this? We must make major changes to our education system, but before we start considering changes we must make, let's review the history of the increased requirement for education.

In medieval times only the clergy and aristocrats were educated. Peasants did not need an education. The clergy and the aristocrats were taught subjects which were needed by them. They studied Latin, literature, including the Bible, French, history,

1

The Changing Workplace

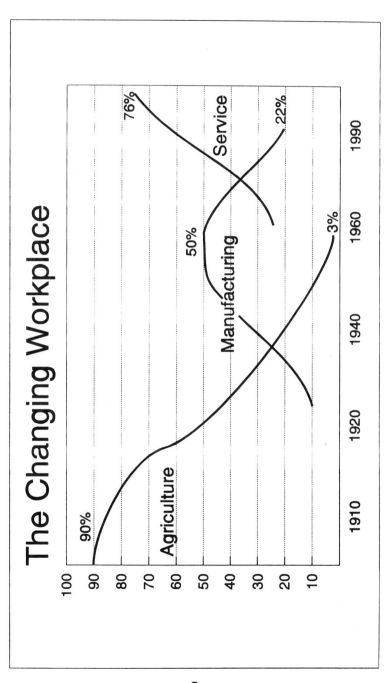

geography as was known at that time, how to read and write, basic arithmetic, manners and courtesy.

As man began to break the yoke of medieval slavery, he found he needed an education in order to be able to survive as a free man. For example, farmers needed to know how to read, write, and cipher in order to operate the farm. The industrial revolution generated a requirement for more education, and began to change us from an agrarian society to an industrialized society. For example, farm machinery began to appear on farms, and knowledge of agriculture began to increase. This created a requirement that farmers be better educated, and that we train more engineers. Land Grant colleges were established to fill the requirement for engineers and knowledgeable farmers. Other colleges soon followed and began to teach agriculture and engineering. This was the beginning of the requirement for more education for everyone.

With the introduction of the computer into our society, a new class of worker was generated - service workers. Introduction of the computer required better educated workers in all fields of endeavor.

The net result of an increasing need for more education is that now the average job requires about two years of education beyond high school. This tells us we must overhaul our public schools in order to be able to take care of the requirement for more education for everyone. The requirement for two years of education beyond high school can be taken care of by junior colleges and technical schools. Most technical schools have curricula based on the needs of industry, but many junior colleges need to tailor their curricula to fit industry requirements. They must reduce courses in the arts, and increase the number of courses in technology.

As a result of our having fallen so far behind in our public schools, industry has found that they must have a training program of their own to teach even the fundamentals such as reading, writing, and arithmetic. Industry is spending millions of dollars each year to teach subjects to new employees which should have been learned by their employees in high schools or in junior colleges. Our education standard is much lower than many people think. We must get on the ball and start turning out high school graduates who can step into a job in industry and be able to read, write and do math problems. High school graduates going on to college must be ready to begin higher learning. Today, many college freshmen and sophomores are taking remedial courses or watered-down college courses.

If junior and senior colleges are going to raise their standards, the standards for high school graduates must be raised. Every high school graduate must be able to read, write, and do mathematical problems at the high school level of the 1940's and 1950's. Many of our high school graduates are only able to perform at about the eighth grade level. This tells us that we are very far behind in our education system, and that we not only have to improve our education system, we must also play catch-up.

We say we must educate everyone, but we can't educate everyone in our traditional schools. Therefore, we must make major changes to our system. We must have academic/technical channels beginning at the sixth grade. At this juncture in the education of a child, every teacher knows whether a child will succeed in traditional education, or whether the child will have a better chance of succeeding in technical channels (electronics, computers, business, health care, etc.). Our schools must provide these channels, if we are going to be able to educate everyone, and be able to compete with the rest of the world that is becoming more and more technical.

Many educators will resist this change, but the change must be made. Today we are turning out many high school graduates who are not prepared for the workplace or college. We must strive to turn out high school graduates who are ready to go to colleges or technical schools, or to go to work. Those who are going to work after high school must have a skill which is in demand in industry. Automobile body mechanics, etc., does not meet this requirement. We need to have educators work with industry personnel to determine what basic education and skills are required for their entry level employees, and we must change to meet these requirements.

Of course, incorporating technical channels will cost more money, but some of it can be recouped by shrinking the academic channel. Also, a future cost will be reduced by reducing the number of people on welfare or in prison where most of the inmates are dropouts. In many cases they were drop-outs because we tried to teach them subjects in which they had no interest, and which would not help them get a job after graduation. Students must be motivated in order to learn. One way to motivate many of them is for them to see a light at the end of the tunnel - a job. Most people on welfare and in prison did not go to high school. Welfare recipients breed welfare recipients. In short we must educate everyone to the maximum of their ability to be educated.

Once we begin to channel students into areas where they can succeed, we must pass a national law which requires that children be in some kind of a school until they are eighteen years old. Such a law will generate a requirement for channels other than academic and technical. In fact, there will probably be two other channels. One will be for the mentally handicapped. This channel must be created because trying to mainstream the mentally handicapped slows the learning of the average and the above average student. Also, it slows the learning of the handicapped, because they are exposed to a level in which they probably cannot succeed. These unfortunate students should be educated at the level of their ability. The other channel to be created will be for incorrigible students. Something like a boot camp will be necessary. We could use the facilities of military bases which have been closed. They would be particularly good for this purpose, because we need to give these students 24-hour supervision. Here the student could be taught to perform semiskilled jobs, manners, courtesy, health and other subjects which even incorrigibles need. In any event, laws should be passed which require school attendance until eighteen years old. This would result in educating everyone to some extent, would keep juveniles off the streets, and would help reduce crime.

We must create these new channels immediately. We are already behind. Conventional educators will resist the creation of technical and academic channels, but we must do this if we are to educate everyone, and educate everyone we must.

There will be more on the creation of technical channels in Chapter XIII "Curricula."

After students graduate from high school, both males and females should be required to serve in a Universal Military Training program for at least a year. This recommendation will be, and now is, a controversial subject which will arouse the anger of most "do-gooders", and, for sure, the American Civil Liberties Union. But, considering the graduates we are now turning out, we must better prepare them for entering society. Military training will do this. Also, most eighteen year old's are not ready to go to college, or to enter the workplace.

Because of the physical limitations, and different training methods which should be used for the females, the sexes should not be mixed during military training.

Military training during the year should be secondary. The trainees should be taught manners, self-respect, respect for others, social manners, common courtesy, tenacity, and other qualities they will need when entering the workplace or college.

We should look at Universal Military Training as being the finishing school for all students before they enter the workplace or college.

CHAPTER II

HOW BAD?

Before we begin to address ways and means of improving our schools, we must understand how far our students have fallen behind on scores which are made on the Scholastic Achievement Tests (SAT), and how far our students have fallen behind when compared to students in other countries of the world.

The chart on the next page shows the combined SAT scores which were made by our students from 1953 through 1994. As you will note, the combined math and verbal scores remained more or less constant until 1963. At that point in time both scores began a rather precipitous drop, and have now leveled off at about 900. We will explore reasons for the decline beginning in 1963 in later chapters of this book. But, for the time being, consider this - 1962 was the year when the Supreme Court ruled out prayer in schools. Also, the following year was the year when the first of the World War II (WWII) "baby boomers", who were raised under the theory of "let them be themselves - don't cross them", started taking the SAT.

The 1960's was also the time when justices began to water- down our judicial system. A life sentence no longer means that the criminal will spend the rest of his life in jail, and a death sentence has almost become impossible to give to even the worst criminals. The justices and many "do-gooders"

SAT Total Scores

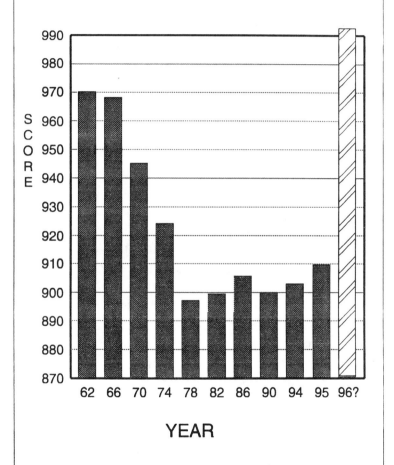

Basic data from the College Entrance Exam Board

10

wanted to try to rehabilitate criminals. Rehabilitation for most hardened criminals is impossible as evidenced by the statistics on repeat offenders. We can't repaint if we haven't painted, and we can't rehabilitate, if we haven't habilitated.

The SAT score did not always reflect the true academic achievement of the taker, but it was the best test that had been devised for many years up through 1995. Now the College Board has changed the scoring on the SAT. The Board calls the change "recentering." The authors call it lowering the standard just as most public school administrators have lowered standards to the point where many high school graduates can't perform at the eighth grade level. In 1996 the recentering will go into effect. At that time recentered SAT scores will be considerably higher than SAT scores were in 1962. We have been using 1962 as a standard for many years. And, based on 1962 scores, we have seen SAT scores drop about 70 points from 1962 to 1995. This drop tells us that today's students are less educated than students were in 1962. With recentering, the scores will tell us that 1996 students are better educated than 1962 students, if we do not use a conversion chart to change the scores back to raw SAT scores. This new scoring system could have been conceived only by a committee composed of educators who were trained to let students set the standards.

The new SAT I will separate students on an academic scale. The SAT II will also separate students on an academic scale, for whatever good that will do.

Some colleges have developed tests of their own which are administered to applicants for admission. These tests are used to supplement the SAT score, or to eliminate the SAT completely. Most of these tests do include essay type tasks which almost everyone would like to include in achievement tests.

Now let's examine how our students stand academically when compared to students in other countries in the world. The charts on the following page show how far our "top" students have fallen behind "top" students from other countries. As you will note, our top students ranked third from the bottom in both science and mathematics. In math our students ranked higher than only two countries - Spain and Jordan. In science our top students scored better than only two countries -Ireland and Jordan. The two countries whose students scored higher than students from all the other countries in both science and math are Korea and Taiwan. What do these charts tell us? They tell us that our future is in jeopardy, because we will not be able to compete in this world which is becoming more and more technically oriented. They also tell us that we must take positive action to change what is being taught in our schools, and how it is being taught.

We have learned how our top students compare with other top students around the world. Now let's examine how much our students really know - the proof of the pudding. Examine the charts on the following pages. These charts reveal how much our students know, or really how little they know.

As the science chart indicates, students at the

fourth grade through the twelfth grade understand simple scientific principles fairly well. But, when asked to apply simple scientific principles, many of them were not able to apply what they know. When asked to analyze scientific principles and data, they failed miserably.

When asked to integrate specialized knowledge, we may as well have asked a barn yard rooster or the stock picking monkey to perform the task. Most students do not possess in-depth scientific knowledge or the ability to accomplish even relatively straight forward tasks requiring application or thinking skills. In math, our students also get an "F". All high school seniors demonstrated success in working with whole numbers, but when asked to multiply and solve simple two-step problems, their scores dropped. Maybe we should have stopped testing at that point, because we had found that most of our high school students were not capable of going beyond multiplication and simple problem solving. However, we did go on, and we found that less than half of the high school students were proficient in reasoning and problem solving using fractions, decimals, percentage, geometry, and algebra. None, to only a very few, could solve problems using geometry, algebra, and statistics.

Now that we have defined the problem, we need to begin to find solutions. In industry, for example, if a company had a cash flow problem, every factor which could affect cash flow would be examined before taking action. Management would look at receipts, receivables, overdue income, pricing, in

HOW U.S. STUDENTS COMPARE INTERNATIONALLY?

SCIENCE ACHIEVEMENT AT AGE 13 -- THE TOP 10 PERCENT

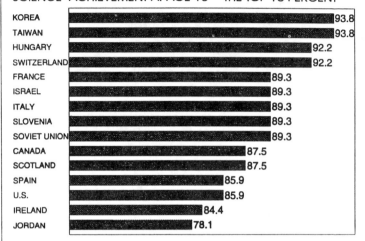

KOREA	93.8
TAIWAN	93.8
HUNGARY	92.2
SWITZERLAND	92.2
FRANCE	89.3
ISRAEL	89.3
ITALY	89.3
SLOVENIA	89.3
SOVIET UNION	89.3
CANADA	87.5
SCOTLAND	87.5
SPAIN	85.9
U.S.	85.9
IRELAND	84.4
JORDAN	78.1

MATHMATICS ACHIEVEMENT AT AGE 13 -- THE TOP 10 PERCENT

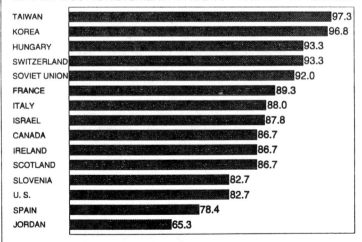

TAIWAN	97.3
KOREA	96.8
HUNGARY	93.3
SWITZERLAND	93.3
SOVIET UNION	92.0
FRANCE	89.3
ITALY	88.0
ISRAEL	87.8
CANADA	86.7
IRELAND	86.7
SCOTLAND	86.7
SLOVENIA	82.7
U. S.	82.7
SPAIN	78.4
JORDAN	65.3

Percentage of science and math questions answered correctly by "top" students from 15 countries. The United States ranked near the bottom in both.

14

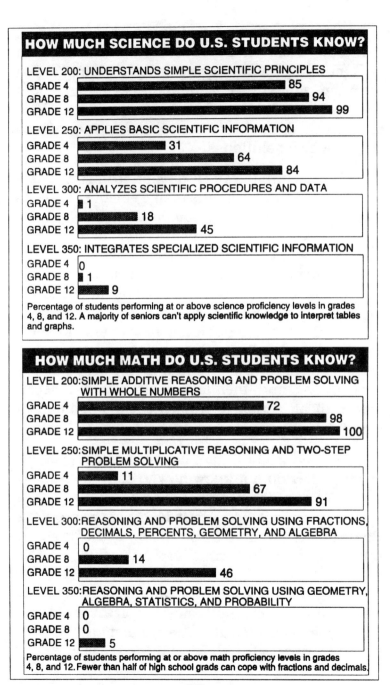

HOW MUCH SCIENCE DO U.S. STUDENTS KNOW?

LEVEL 200: UNDERSTANDS SIMPLE SCIENTIFIC PRINCIPLES

GRADE 4	85
GRADE 8	94
GRADE 12	99

LEVEL 250: APPLIES BASIC SCIENTIFIC INFORMATION

GRADE 4	31
GRADE 8	64
GRADE 12	84

LEVEL 300: ANALYZES SCIENTIFIC PROCEDURES AND DATA

GRADE 4	1
GRADE 8	18
GRADE 12	45

LEVEL 350: INTEGRATES SPECIALIZED SCIENTIFIC INFORMATION

GRADE 4	0
GRADE 8	1
GRADE 12	9

Percentage of students performing at or above science proficiency levels in grades 4, 8, and 12. A majority of seniors can't apply scientific knowledge to interpret tables and graphs.

HOW MUCH MATH DO U.S. STUDENTS KNOW?

LEVEL 200: SIMPLE ADDITIVE REASONING AND PROBLEM SOLVING WITH WHOLE NUMBERS

GRADE 4	72
GRADE 8	98
GRADE 12	100

LEVEL 250: SIMPLE MULTIPLICATIVE REASONING AND TWO-STEP PROBLEM SOLVING

GRADE 4	11
GRADE 8	67
GRADE 12	91

LEVEL 300: REASONING AND PROBLEM SOLVING USING FRACTIONS, DECIMALS, PERCENTS, GEOMETRY, AND ALGEBRA

GRADE 4	0
GRADE 8	14
GRADE 12	46

LEVEL 350: REASONING AND PROBLEM SOLVING USING GEOMETRY, ALGEBRA, STATISTICS, AND PROBABILITY

GRADE 4	0
GRADE 8	0
GRADE 12	5

Percentage of students performing at or above math proficiency levels in grades 4, 8, and 12. Fewer than half of high school grads can cope with fractions and decimals.

15

ventory, and any other factors which could affect cash flow. Then management would examine each one until they found the one or ones which needed attention. After this examination, solutions would be arrived at which would solve the problem. Then, and only then, would management determine which were the best solutions.

School administrators do not go through this process. They did not take management courses in college. There they were taught theoretical education courses, none of which would help them to administer and manage schools. Most of them are so inadequate at problem solving that they don't even know how to take the first step - definition of the problem. And, even if they did take this first step, most of them would not know how to take the next step -list down all possible solutions; then select the one, or ones, which would be the best solution or solutions; and, then take positive, and, if necessary radical, action to implement the solution or solutions.

Since "educators" have not been taught problem solving, they do not know how to solve their problems. Some of them do not even know they have a problem, or will not admit to having a problem. Some of them want to throw money at the problem; others want to find some way of teaching so that students learn through osmosis; some want to find ways to pour knowledge into students; some think we need to keep putting band-aids on the problems; and some are satisfied if the students are just exposed to knowledge. None of these are viable solutions. They have all been tried without success. Now is the time to take immediate and drastic actions in order to turn the problem around. The actions we must take are:

1. Start children to school at the age of three.
2. Limit bilingual education.
3. Adopt English as our official language.
4. Teach values in school.
5. Train teachers to be motivator, father, mother, counselor, and confidant to their students.
6. Select principals and superintendents based on their ability to control their schools, not on courses they have taken.
7. Use corporal punishment in schools.
8. Have a national ironclad law which requires mandatory school attendance until eighteen years old.
9. Realize that there will be failures.
10. Have separate academic/technical channels beginning at the sixth grade.
11. Have work camps for those who have not reached the age of eighteen, have dropped out of school, and are roaming the streets.
12. Make our students be proud that they are an American.
13. Have more college scholarships for the underprivileged who are capable of pursuing technical courses in college.
14. Have abbreviated science and math courses

for students who do not take standard high school math and science courses.

15. Demand that all teachers be able to teach abbreviated math and science courses.

16. Eliminate or reduce the number of courses given in state supported colleges which do not prepare students to make a living from what they have learned. Conversely, we must expand technical, science, trade, and math courses.

17. Have year-round schools.

18. Have after school programs.

19. Use retired military personnel, teachers who want extra pay, and honor students to conduct after school activities.

20. Recognize that our national educational level will determine our economic level and the future of our nation.

21. Fire teachers who cannot motivate.

22. Raise the standard for teachers and pay them better.

23. Recognize that the degree of poverty is directly related to the educational level which students attain.

24. Recognize that it costs nine times more to keep a person in prison than it does to educate a person.

25. Have authority to garnishee pay checks for child support.

26. Require students to wear uniforms to school.

27. Rewrite history books so that students will learn history the way it happened - not as we would like for it to have happened.

28. Emphasize the teaching of world geography and history.

29. Abolish education degrees.

30. Set a goal of a 50/50 ratio of male/female teachers.

31. Get industry involved in course development.

32. Add college and industry personnel to State Education Agencies, and eliminate the drones in these agencies.

33. Provide room and board schools for some disadvantaged students.

34. Recognize there is no easy way to teach. Knowledge cannot be poured into the students.

35. Recognize that knowledge available to us doubles every twelve years.

36. Recognize that all of us must be better educated.

37. Build burglar-proof fences around some of our schools.

38. Recognize that poor education is more deadly than an atomic bomb.

39. Change adult and juvenile laws to more closely resemble the old "an eye for an eye, a tooth for a tooth" punishment.

40. Teach our teachers how to maintain discipline.

41. Teach our teachers how to get parents involved.

42. Relieve teachers of the heavy burden of paper work.

43. Get teachers involved in curricula development.

44. Provide recovery centers for every drug addict.

45. Separate the sexes beginning at the sixth grade.

46. Make changes to college courses for students who want to become teachers.

47. Eventually eliminate school boards.

48. Provide vouchers for some students.

49. Educate all students to the maximum of their ability.

50. Last, but not least, reverse the Supreme Court ruling concerning prayer in schools.

That's quite a list of things we must do. Everyone of them must be accomplished, and ways to do this will be addressed in this book. But, before we leave this chapter, let's address the question everyone is asking:

WHY CAN'T JOHNNY READ, WRITE, OR DO ARITHMETIC PROBLEMS?

This is the question which everyone is asking, and the answer is a very simple one - Johnny hasn't been taught to read, write, and do arithmetic problems. How can we make a statement like that? We can because it is a fact that reading, writing, and doing arithmetic problems must be taught. So, if the students haven't learned to do these things, can we assume that the teachers haven't taught? The answer is an emphatic NO. We can't say that teachers haven't taught, because most of them work their hearts out trying to teach their students. A few of the reasons the students haven't learned are: they haven't come to school ready to learn; they have not been motivated, taught values, and disciplined at home; some teachers, principals, and administrators are not qualified for their positions; and the environment in many schools is not conducive to learning. Changes must be made in the home and in many schools before we can get education back on track. The old adage "If the students haven't learned, the teacher hasn't taught" no longer holds true.

Let's start with why Johnny can't read. Reading should start with the mother and father reading to their children. How many parents do this? Not very many. Reading to a child by the parents inspires their children to learn more about their new world. Children will want to be able to read like their parents can read. The child will want to do this, because all children want to grow up being like their parents. If the parents read, the child will want to read. If the parents fight, the child will be aggressive, and will probably grow up to be a spouse or child abuser. If the parents love each other, the child will learn to love. All children want to be like their parents.

Since all parents do not teach their children to read, and they can be taught how to read by the parents, we must find some other way to teach them to read. This can be done by starting all children to school at the age of three. In the three year old's school, we must begin instruction in English with the ABC's. Once the child has memorized the alphabet, and has learned to pronounce the letters correctly, we can begin to teach reading by putting the letters together to teach the child to read simple one syllable words like cat, hat, bat, etc. As soon as the child has been taught how to read one syllable words, we can begin teaching how to read words with two or more syllables. We do this by teaching the child how to pronounce each syllable. At this time we should begin teaching phonics, because the child will not be able to pronounce all syllables, if phonics have not been taught.

In many schools today, children are taught sight reading. This is the method Dr. Gallaudet used to teach the deaf, because they could not hear. Most children do not have a hearing problem and must be taught phonics, if we want them to learn to read English. If we were teaching reading in Spanish, all we would have to do is teach the student the correct pronunciation of the Spanish alphabet. The child would then be ready to start reading, because all words in Spanish are pronounced like they are spelled. Not so in English. If phonics is not taught in the first grade where reading is being taught, the children in that school will never be able to read and understand at a rate that is required in today's world.

If you are a parent, and have a child who is having trouble reading, go before the School Board and demand that phonics be taught. If this effort fails, take the child out of the school and enroll the child in a private school where phonics is taught, or teach phonics at home. Remember, if children can't read, they cannot learn enough to complete school, and will end up on welfare or in prison.

Now let's address writing. A child must be able to read before we can teach writing. While the child is being taught how to read and write, we can begin to teach how to spell. But a child cannot be taught how to read, write, and spell, if the child has not been taught phonics. Without phonetic training, a child will not be able to learn to spell, or to look up a word in the dictionary or encyclopedia. If the child can't spell, how can the child learn to write? A child must have a command of words in order to put together a proper sentence, and no one has a command of words in the English language, if one does not have a knowledge of phonics. It's foolish to try to teach writing, reading, and spelling, if the child is not given phonics training.

The English language is one of the most difficult languages to learn. It is also one of the most rewarding languages to use, because English has more words which can be used to express our feelings, ideas, or message. The number of descriptive words which English has to offer is one reason why English is being adopted as the universal language of commerce, diplomacy, medicine, science, and control of air and sea travel. But, as has been said, it is a difficult language to learn, and it cannot be learned without phonics training.

Now let's explore why Johnny can't do arithmetic problems. The same reasoning applies in arithmetic as in reading and writing. The child must be taught and taught properly. A child can't learn to add by casting out nines, or using a calculator. The child must learn to add any two numbers together. After the child has learned to add two numbers, we must teach how to add three or more numbers together by memory. Why does the child have to learn to add by memory? Let's use an example. If a person goes to the grocery store and wants to buy three oranges priced at 25 cents each, the buyer must be able to add 25¢ to 25¢ to 25¢ or be able to multiply from memory. If people can't do this from memory, they are mathematics illiterates.

In order to be able to multiply, a child must memorize the multiplication tables. How does a child memorize the tables? By doing them over and over until they are committed to memory. This sounds like rote, and it is - but there is no other way. If a teacher allows a child to pass the subject of multi-plication without committing the tables to memory, the teacher is violating a basic principle of teaching mathematics, and should be relieved of teaching math.

The child will not be able to do division problems, if the child does not know how many threes there are in the number nine, for example. In order to teach division, the child must learn to determine how many X's there are in the numbers one through nine. If the child does not memorize this, the child will never be able to do division. How does the child learn this? There is only one way, and that way is to do the problems over and over until the task is learned. Call it rote, if you want to, but it is the only way. A calculator is for persons who have already mastered basic math. It is not for anyone trying to learn basic mathematics. The calculator must be taken out of the public schools for any subjects short of calculus. If we continue to let students use the calculator, we will continue to turn out mathematics illiterates.

After the child has been taught how to add, subtract, multiply, and divide, we must teach fractions and decimals. We must teach this so that a child will have a good foundation in arithmetic. All children need a good foundation in arithmetic before going into higher mathematics such as algebra, geometry, trigonometry and calculus, and they are not prepared to study these subjects if they do not understand fractions and decimals.

Before we leave why Johnny can't read, write, or do math, let's explore some of the reasons, really excuses, that "educators" use to cover up their failures to teach Johnny. One of the favorite excuses is that Johnny has Dyslexia. Some children have a learning disability, but the disability must be diagnosed by a physician, and cannot be diagnosed by a teacher. Many school districts will put a child in the category of learning disabled because the district gets federal money for the learning disabled. Most

25

children do not have a learning disability, but many schools have a teaching disability. For example, trying to teach reading, writing, and spelling without teaching phonics. Another example, is not requiring students to memorize multiplication tables, simple addition, division problems, fractions, and decimals. If we are going to let students use calculators in school, we don't need to teach arithmetic and mathematics, all we need to do is teach the student how to read the directions which come with the calculator.

In conclusion, don't blame the teachers for Johnny's not being able to read, write, and do arithmetic problems. Blame the parents, teacher colleges and school administrators. There will be much more on teachers, administrators, and teacher trainers in later chapters.

Teaching in public schools has become so bad that:

1. The United States has dropped to 49th in world literacy.

2. Approximately 61% of 17 year-olds can't read at high school level.

3. Our colleges have had to lower their standards so they can accept semi-illiterates into their schools.

If these statistics don't scare you into action, nothing will. It's later than you think - get yourself onto the fast track and get going.

HOW BAD IS IT? ANSWER - IT CAN'T GET ANY WORSE, WE HOPE.

CHAPTER III

FAMILY

As was stated in the introduction, the decline of the family was listed as the number one cause of the deterioration of our schools. In this chapter we are going to review the history of the family and list the factors which contributed to the family's downfall. Also, we are going to cover the importance of having the families involved in the education of their children at home and in the schools their children are attending. But, first let's review the history of the family.

In the very early days of man and woman, they lived in tribes. Living together in tribes was the way they protected themselves from wild animals, from other tribes, and the way they satisfied their urge to socialize. However, this living arrangement afforded many other advantages. Man's hunting was more successful because he hunted in numbers. They learned cooperation and respect for others, and their self-respect was developed. They were cared for when they were no longer able to do their tribal duties, and the children were educated in the skills which were necessary for their survival.

Chores in the tribe were divided among the members who were best qualified for the tribal duties. The women prepared the food; taught the children what they needed to know before adulthood; wove fabrics for clothes; and cared for the elderly. Both the boys and the girls were taught the same skills until the boys were old enough to go on hunts with the men. Living in tribes was very nearly an ideal way for mankind to live. Their survival was assured, and they knew that they would be cared for when they were too old to perform tribal tasks.

As the numbers in the tribe grew, some of the members became dissatisfied and left the tribe. They always left in pairs - a man and a woman. Probably all of us remember seeing a cartoon of a cave man dragging a cave woman by her hair to his new lair. That wasn't the way it happened. There was always a woman who was willing to leave the tribe and go with the man. Thank goodness for that! When they started living together as man and wife, children came, but they didn't know why they were having children. They were not even curious - they were too busy trying to survive. We must remember that the knowledge of the miracle of child birth was not known until many, many centuries later. Even Renaissance man believed that the woman was only an incubator, and that the child was his and his only.

As the man and woman left the tribe and started a family, it soon became apparent that families needed each other. So, they started living closer together. Proximity afforded better protection and also provided many other advantages. For example, they could hunt in numbers; they could help each other erect shelters; they could share the chore of educating the children; they could share the responsibility of caring for the elderly; and many other chores which were necessary. As the number of families living close to each other grew, small villages began to appear.

The size of the early families was limited by the amount of food they could produce, and by the high infant and child death rate caused by malnutrition and disease. When the plow was invented their living conditions and their health changed for the better. The families could produce more food, and they became better nourished. This allowed them to raise more children, and more children were needed to help with plowing and harvesting. This marked the beginning of the population growth of the human race. The growth is continuing and is fast becoming a problem, because we cannot produce enough food for the numbers we now have. We are not able to feed all of our present population for two reasons; one, the problem of transporting food does not have a solution; and two, if all of the arable land in the world were cultivated to its maximum potential, we could not produce enough food. That's a sad situation which is becoming worse. The problem is becoming worse, because we are producing more people every day, and land which was arable is becoming less productive and is being lost through erosion. Loss of up to forty tons of top soil from every acre in some areas is occurring. Also, lowering of the water table in the whole world is a contributing factor.

No one has found a solution to the overpopulation problem. We will have to become accustomed to people dying from hunger and malnutrition. We must do all we can to alleviate this terrible problem, but we are working on the wrong end of the problem - feeding the hungry. We need to do this, but we must start working on the other end of the problem - birth control.

As farming became more efficient, and as the size of the family grew, some of the children who were no longer needed on the farm moved to the towns to work there. This happened about the time of the industrial revolution. As a result of increasing industry, many products were produced which improved the living conditions of the families. This was the beginning of the desire for material things. The desire for material things has contributed to the downfall of many families. Some parents are more interested in having two automobiles, two TV sets, a house with a family room and two or more baths than they are in teaching values to their children. The desire for material things caused many women to go to work. In fact, some of the working women make only enough to pay for baby sitting, the clothes they wear to work, and payments on the automobile they drive to work. Too many women have abdicated their God-given role of mother to their children. They fill the role of bearer of the children, but go off to work and let someone else raise the children.

Women going to work flooded the labor market with more workers than employers needed, so they did not have to pay high salaries to the men they employed. This resulted in lowering wages to a point where a man could not support a family. Some of these problems could be solved by a family living in a smaller house, and doing with fewer material things. Prior to WWII most families lived in houses with few amenities, two or more children to a room, and only one bath. It can be done again, but many families put material things above the raising of their children.

Prior to, and immediately after WWII, families taught values to their children. They taught the Ten Commandments (or equivalent) and the Golden Rule. This value training was also taught in public and private schools. The result was that when children left home to live on their own, they were well-equipped to live in a moral society which they found in the outside world. Value training in the home and in the schools continued until the Supreme Court ruled that prayers could not be said in public schools. This marked the end of moral training in schools, which contributed to the decline of moral training in the home. However, prior to the ruling of the Supreme Court we saw the beginning of the family where both parents worked.

When we began to train young men for World War II, there became a shortage of men to produce the arms necessary to win the war. So, young women started working in defense plants or anywhere they were needed. Those who worked in aircraft and war machine factories were affectionately called "Rosie the Riveter". These women and older men were the ones who produced the war machinery in quantities which were necessary for our fighting men to win the war. So, we must give credit not only to "GI Joe", but also to "Rosie the Riveter" and all the other men and women who supported the war effort.

When the war was over, GI Joe came home and married Rosie the Riveter. The GI Joe's had no training to work in the peacetime world, so many took advantage of the "GI Bill" to go to college or to a trade school to learn a skill. The Bill provided enough money for Joe to live on, but not enough for both of them to live on. What was the solution? Rosie went to work again. This was the beginning of the family where both the man and the woman worked.

Of course they began to raise a family while both of them continued to work. When both parents work they do not have enough time to properly raise children. Raising children requires the devotion of a full-time mother, and a father who works and provides for the family. The Creator designed woman to perform the most challenging job of mankind - producing and raising children. There is no other job more important in this world.

At about the same time Joe and Rosie began raising a family, a "let them raise themselves" philosophy was being touted. The philosophy was based on the flawed theory that children must be allowed to "do their thing" during their childhood, otherwise they will grow up and not be able to express themselves and have a free and open mind. We all know that such a theory is as wrong as any theory can be. A child must be taught right from wrong, self-respect, respect for others, and to obey authority. If children are not taught values all of their young lives, they will grow up to be semi-barbarians. If anyone doubts this, one needs to start reading the newspapers and listening to news casts on TV.

The "let them raise themselves" theory suited Joe and Rosie, because they didn't have enough time to devote to their children. This was the beginning of some children entering the real world with little or no value or disciplinary training.

In the 1962-63 era, Joe's and Rosie's children graduated from high school and started taking the Standard Achievement Test - SAT- for entry into college. The scores were about 971 then and had been that for many of the prior years. So we see that Joe and Rosie's children who were graduated in the early 1960's were holding their own in the academic world. Also, their children had some value training at home and in the schools. Many of Joe's and Rosie's children grew up to be responsible adults. They were a credit to their parents.

However, in the 1962-63 era, the wheels began to come off the wagon. The Supreme Court ruled out prayer in public schools. As soon as this ruling became effective, schools stopped all value training. Also, at this time we started to see the beginning of the change in the family composition, and of the family's lack of value training and control of their children. As a result of the Supreme Court's ruling, and the changes in composition of the family, a downhill slide in education and a decrease in overall morality of our citizens began.

Also, in about the same time frame, our justice

system began to fail to punish criminals with punishment which they deserved. For example, we had the "Lindbergh" law which required the death penalty for kidnapping. We punished murderers with hanging or life in prison. Such punishment has been abandoned. In fact, the laws have been watered-down so much that today our laws ignore the victims and favor the criminals. Our jails are full, and the crime rate continues to climb, because "do-gooders" want to try to rehabilitate the criminal. As we stated in Chapter II, we can't repaint if we haven't painted. Likewise, we can't rehabilitate, if we haven't habilitated, and this we haven't done. We must find a way to reduce the crime rate. A violent crime is committed every two seconds, and a murder is committed every two minutes.

As a result of the Supreme Court's ruling out prayer in schools, little or no value training in the home, and loosening of our laws and morals, the following changes began to take place:

- SAT scores began to decrease
- The divorce rate increased
- Teenage sex and child bearing increased
- Violent crimes increased
- Sexually transmitted diseases increased
(See charts at the end of this chapter)

SAT SCORES
The SAT chart at the end of this chapter shows that SAT scores were fairly consistent until 1963. They began to drop at about that time, and are now

leveling off at about 900 - a drop of about 70 points. This drop reflects the fact that our students are graduating with fewer academic skills than pre-1963 graduates. This is the first time in history when the new generation is less educated than the previous generation. Some high school graduates can't read at the eighth grade level, and nearly all colleges have had to develop remedial courses.

DIVORCE RATE

The divorce rate has increased dramatically since 1963 as indicated by the divorce rate chart at the end of this chapter. When parents divorce before their children have finished school and have left home, their children are very adversely affected. The children feel that they have been robbed of their birth right - having both a father and a mother. Generally custody of the children is given to the mother. She tries to make a living for the family, to give the children love and affection, and to give them moral training, but most often she fails. She fails, because raising a family and making a living are both full-time jobs. No one can do both and be successful at both.

TEENAGE SEX AND CHILD BEARING

The lack of moral training in the home, the "sexual revolution", the high divorce rate, the "pill", the Women's Rights Movement, and moral decline caused the teenagers to use their bodies promiscuously. The results were an increase in the number of unwed mothers, an increase in sexually transmitted diseases, and an increase in school dropouts. In 1993 the cost to support unwed mothers and their children was 35 billion dollars. One out of every three children born, is born to an unwed mother. How long will the tax payers continue supporting unwed mothers and their children?

VIOLENT CRIMES

Violent crime has increased tremendously since 1963 compared to the population growth. It has risen from about 250,000 offenses in the 1961-62 era to about 1,700,000 in 1989-90 era. The causes for the rise in the crime rate are many, but the primary cause is that our justice system and families have failed us. The saddest part of the problem is that teenagers are responsible for much of the increase in crime. Children are killing children and others.

SEXUALLY TRANSMITTED DISEASE

The rate of increase in sexually transmitted diseases has risen dramatically since 1963. In 1963 there were about 14 cases per 100,000. In 1989 their were about 45 cases per 100,000.

The increase in the divorce rate marked the increase in one parent families. This resulted in less and less teaching of moral values at home. Single parent families have been the principal cause for the huge increases in immorality which is reflected in the charts at the end of this chapter. Our jails are filled to overflowing and we can't build jails fast enough to incarcerate all of the criminals. Therefore, we have a revolving door prison system. We let them out on the streets before they have served their time. This lets the criminal commit another crime before he goes back to prison. We must strengthen our laws, and revert to an "eye for an eye, and a tooth for a tooth" type of punishment for hardened criminals.

The pre-WWII family no longer exists, so we have to work with the family we have. In most cases, both parents work, or the family has only one parent - usually a mother who is divorced or who never had a husband. As has been said before, children need the love and affection of both a father who works, and a mother who does not work and who devotes her entire time to raising the children.

Children, from the time they are born until they go to school, need a full-time mother. When the children are infants the mother needs to breast-feed her children and to hold them close to her. This gives confidence the child needs to have in this strange new world into which the child was born. Also, the mother needs to read while holding the child. This gives the child a great deal of learning while still an infant, and it creates a desire to learn more. This will motivate the child to learn to read, and a child can be taught to read much earlier than most of us thought. It's a sad fact that one out of five mothers can't read. We must correct this problem by literacy training for all parents who can't read or write.

A child must be held close to the mother's breast until it can take solid food, and must be loved and disciplined by the mother and father. It is now theorized that the child's brain will not develop as it should in the early years of it's life, if the child is not held close to the mother until the child can walk. The damage to the brain is thought to be permanent and cannot be repaired. The child will go through life with this handicap.

Now let's go forward to the time when children become students in high school. Here they need to be taught the facts of life about marriage and the opposite sex. They need to know that each sex is different. Why are they different? They are different because the Creator designed them to perform different jobs. In fact they are so different they could have come from different planets. They think differently, they talk differently, they reason differently, they have different goals in life, they even use different sides of their brain. The description of their differences is unending. Women in the Women's Liberation Movement will not admit to this, but it is a fact. There is a path between the two sides of the brain, but it is not wide enough for either sex to change their characteristics from one sex to another. However, the female has one advantage over the male in the crossover between the two parts of the brain. The crossover in the female permits her to use both sides of the brain for communicating. Maybe that is why the female has more to say than a male.

The Unisex theory is flawed. However, the Women's Movement has accomplished one thing - some women do not know how to be a woman and a mother, and some men do not know how to be a man, a provider, and a father. Wake up women - do

38

what you were placed on this earth to do - which is to reproduce, and to raise the product of your reproduction - your children. Wake up men - do what you were put on this earth to do - provide for the children who you helped to create, love the mother of your children, and provide for the family. Stop being a Wimp.

If men and women are so different, how did the Creator expect them to get together and populate the world? He gave each of them hormones and physical characteristics which would attract each other like a powerful magnet.

He gave the woman hormones which make her want to "create in her own image". A woman will go to whatever ends are necessary for her to fulfill this God-given mission. If she goes through her child bearing years and does not have a child, she will regret this the rest of her life. Her hormones cause her to seek out a man to provide the seed for creation, and one who could support her and their children. God gave hormones to the male which make him want to be a part of the creation process. However, his sexual hormones are much stronger than the sexual hormones of the female, and he will go to whatever ends are necessary to satisfy his sexual needs. He is attracted to every female who looks good to him, and most females do look good to him. This attraction will continue for his lifetime, and in his later years he will be called a "dirty old man", because he looks at good looking women. Women should understand this and learn to cope with it. High school students should be taught these and other things about man and woman such as anatomy, family planning, family finances, etc. No student should be graduated from high school who has not been taught the facts of life, love, marriage, and child raising.

The female hormones cause the woman to always look at a man with this thought in mind - would he make a good father? So, during her youth, she surveys the field with the intention of selecting a man to be the father of her children. On the other hand, the young man looks at every female as a sexual partner. Eventually he narrows the field down to one he would like to have as his wife, and the mother of his children. At that time male and female get together and start raising a family. They will have differences about many things including how often they want to have sex, but with time they will be able to adjust to a routine which will satisfy both of them.

The chemistry which got them together will hold them together for a time. Their children will become a part of the holding together process, and become a complement to the chemistry. However, if true love does not replace the sexual attraction, the children alone will not hold them together. From the time a couple is married, they must begin to try to change sexual attraction to true love. This can be done only if both practice self-respect, respect for each other, concern for their children, love of life, and sharing of goals for the family. During this period the husband should remember that his wife needs the love of her husband. She must be treated with respect

40

and be loved. She needs to be hugged and kissed every day - not once in a while, or when the husband wants to have sex. She will need this all of her life. Husbands you need to send flowers to your wife, and take her dancing. Also, you need to have a joint bank account.

On the other hand the wife needs to know that her husband may want sex when she does not. She has the ability to accommodate her husband, and she has the ability to "fake it". Also, she needs to recognize that her husband needs to know that he is fulfilling his God-given mission of providing for and loving the family he helped create. The wife can do this by giving a little praise now and then. If true love does not replace the chemistry, then they will divorce. When this happens, they become a part of the problem we are experiencing in educating and teaching morals to our children.

While we are on the subject of educating men and women about their differences, and what they must do to stay together as husband and wife, let's give a little more advise. We will start with advise to the men and then to the women in the following paragraphs.

If you are a man and want a family, you must first be a man - not a Wimp. By being a man, we don't mean a macho man who controls the purse strings, we mean a man who loves his family, and shares a joint bank account and all that he has with his wife. He must have his family foremost in his mind at all times, and he must love and protect them. He must remember that he is the male role model for his sons and his daughters.

He must remember that every woman is a romantic. She wants to love and be loved. If you don't love her, someone else will, or your family will be broken by divorce. She is the one who reads love stories, watches soap operas, and has romantic dreams and desires of her own. You must become a part of her romantic dreams.

A woman is much more vocal than a man. Therefore, you must listen to her and try to understand what she is saying. She may have a message for you clothed in some of her many words.

The average woman is no more beautiful than the average man is handsome. But every woman wants to do everything she can to be as beautiful as she can be. She does this in order to make her feel good, to attract men or a man, to be the envy of other women, and to secretly hope that a pass will be made. In order to make herself more attractive, she will do everything she can to her face and body. She will also dress, down-dress, or undress as necessary. (Women are sometimes torn between the decision to dress or undress.)

In summary, the husband must understand his wife, and do everything he can to make her happy. She will be happy, if you treat her with respect and truly love her.

A wife must do everything she can to keep her husband happy. She can do this in many ways. First, she must tell her husband that she loves him and what a great guy he is. Husbands will thrive on flattery. They also thrive on things the wife can do such as:

1. Greet him when he comes home from work.
2. Make the house a home and a refuge.
3. Keep herself attractive.
4. Keep order among the children.
5. Keep the family financially solvent.
6. Have some interest in some activity that the whole family, including the children, can have an interest in.
7. Keep him sexually satisfied,

Some families do stay together without the advise which was given in the preceding paragraphs, and create a traditional family where the father works and the mother stays at home to raise the children. However, this kind of family is in the minority. A single parent, or a family with two working parents, does not have enough time to teach values to their children. As a result, children come to school with little or no moral training, and many are not motivated to learn. This causes disciplinary problems in the schools and slows the teaching process for those students who have had moral training at home and are motivated to learn. In addition to causing a problem at school, children who are raised in a one parent family cannot grow up to be a whole person. They have not experienced a father who disciplines and loves, and a mother who loves and cares for them. They will have difficulty in adjusting to married life because the boys in the family have not had a father as a good role model. Therefore, when the boy marries, he has not had the experience which is provided by a loving, caring family, and a father who is a man in every sense of the word. In short, the boy does not know how to be the man of the family. Girls in the family also have a problem. They don't know how to treat their husband, and how to be a traditional mother. They are not prepared to adjust to family life where a father leads and a mother follows. These young parents will probably divorce, and may become violent before they separate.

We cannot change this situation, but we can hold parents responsible for the education of their children both at home and in the school. How do we do this? It won't be easy, but it must be done. The first thing we need to do is require the parents to know what their children should be learning in school. How do we do this? We prepare an outline of what is being taught in their child's grade level. Then we tell the parents that they are going to be responsible for their child's learning of the subject material. This will involve insuring that their children attend school every day and that they do their homework. Also, the parents should be required to check on the progress of their children by talking to the teachers of their children. This should be done periodically, and parents should not wait for the teachers to call them. If parents do not follow-up on the progress of their children's education, they may find that it is too late for corrective action when they discover the problem.

Parents must also be required to attend a lecture on school polices, etc., before their children can be entered into school each year. This will ensure that parents, students, and school officials start off on the same wave length. After the presentation, parents should be required to sign a form which states that they understand the school's rules and regulations, and that they will be held responsible for their child's education and their behavior in and out of school.

If parents fail to hold up their end of the responsibility for educating their children, the parents must be forced to do this by law. They must be jailed, if their children are truants, or if their children cannot be controlled in school. This sounds harsh, but we cannot continue to let children be disruptive in school and not do their homework. We can't change the composition of the family, but we can make all parents responsible for their children. This has been done in some school districts, and can be done in all.

We must not let a woman become an incubator, have a child, and then go back to work as soon as the baby is dry. We need a hiring policy which frowns on hiring any woman who has a child at home who is less than three years old. At three, a child can be sent to kindergarten to begin learning how to get along with other children, to learn right from wrong, and to begin to learn about the "three R's."

Another thing we should do to help the family is to make it impossible for a couple to divorce until all children are eighteen years old or older. If they separate during the child raising period, the children must be supported financially. We can do this by red-flagging the Social Security number of the parent who is responsible for child support. Then the employer can withhold the amount of money the parent is to pay, if the parent dose not pay voluntarily.

In summary, we find that decline in composition and morality of the family is a major factor in the decline of our education system, and the morality of our nation. That, combined with the Supreme Court's ruling out prayer in schools, is the combination which has put our nation on the path to ruin.

THE HUMAN ANIMAL IS THE MOST DIFFICULT TO RAISE OF ALL THE ANIMALS IN THE WORLD. A FULL TIME MOTHER AND FATHER IS REQUIRED FOR ABOUT EIGHTEEN YEARS TO PROPERLY RAISE AN OFFSPRING, AND PARENTS ARE NOT TRAINED FOR THE JOB. WE MUST BEGIN PARENTHOOD TRAINING IN OUR HIGH SCHOOLS.

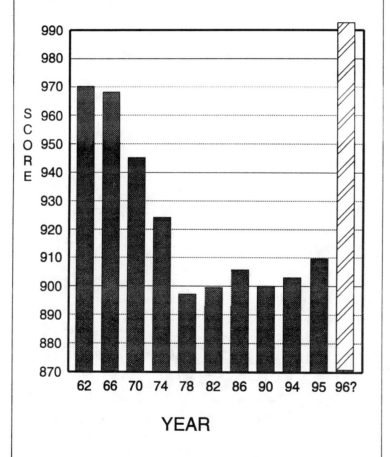

SAT Total Scores

Basic data from the College Entrance Exam Board

47

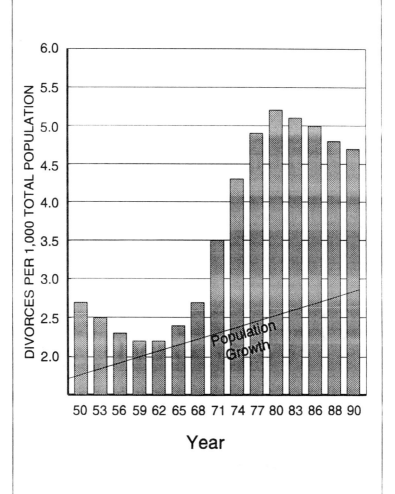

Divorce Rates

DIVORCES PER 1,000 TOTAL POPULATION

Population Growth

Year

50 53 56 59 62 65 68 71 74 77 80 83 86 88 90

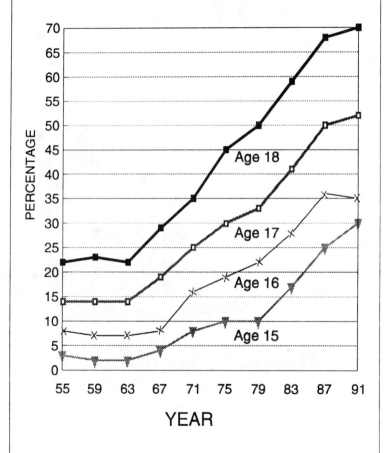

Pre-Marital Sex

Percentage of U.S. Teenage Girls
Who Have Had Pre-Marital Intercourse

Age 18

Age 17

Age 16

Age 15

YEAR

PERCENTAGE

Basic data from Family Planning Perspectives, and from
Sexual and Reproductive Behavior of American Women

49

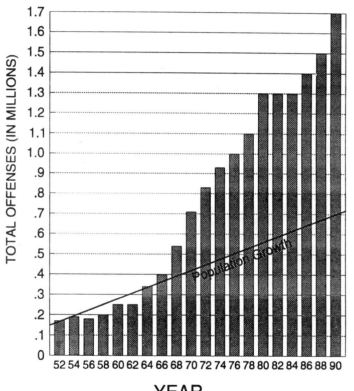

Violent Crime: Number Of Offenses

Basic data from Statistical Abstracts of the United States, and the Department of Commerce, Census Bureau.

Cases Of Sexually Transmitted Diseases

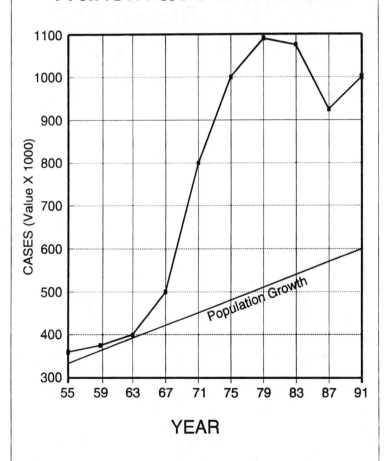

Basic data from Department of Health and Human Services, the Center for Disease Control, and the department of Commerce, Census Bureau.

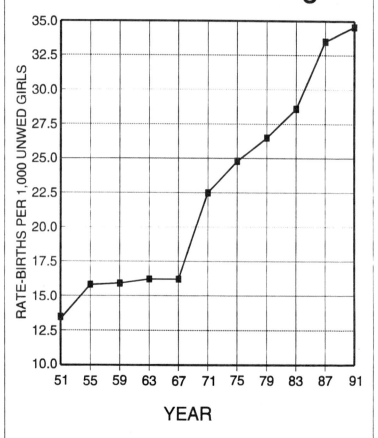

Birth Rates
For Unwed Girls
15 - 19 Years Of Age

Basic data from Department of Health and Human Services and
Statistical Abstracts of the United States.

52

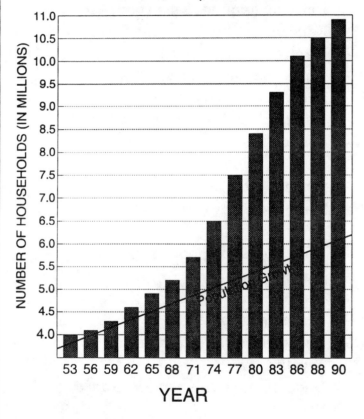

Single Parent
Households
Female Head, No spouse Present

Basic data from Statistical Abstracts of the United States, and the Department of Commerce, Census Bureau.

A B C'S FOR STUDENTS
{Also for all of us}

A - Action, take some

B - Believe in yourself

C - Commitment to your goals

D - Determination to reach your goals

E - Education - get all you can

F - Family - get them involved

G - Goals - set them early

H - Help - get all you can

I - Insist on nothing less than the best

J - Just do it

K - Keep on trying

L - Learn all you can

M - Make every day count

N - Never stop trying

O - Open doors to opportunity

P - Persevere

Q - Quit - never

R - Realize your potential

S - Show the world you can do it

T - Try, try, try

U - Understand where you are headed

V - Values

W - Hard work

X - X out the non productive

Y - Yes, you can

Z - Zero in on your goals

CHAPTER IV

GOALS 2000: EDUCATE AMERICA ACT

During the administration of past President Bush, AMERICA 2000: An Educational Strategy was established. This strategy defined six goals which were to be attained by the year 2000. From this beginning, the GOALS 2000: Educate America Act,was formulated by President Clinton and the US Secretary of Education, Richard W. Riley. The Act was passed by a huge bipartisan House and Senate vote. The Act was signed by President Clinton on 31 March 1994. The Act incorporated the six goals established by AMERICA 2000, and added two more for a total of eight.

The Act also establishes a National Education Goals Panel. This panel is composed of seven governors, two U.S. senators, two U.S. representatives, three state senators, one state representative, the U.S. Secretary of Education, and the President's assistant for domestic policy. Quite an august body. This panel will prepare annual reports on the progress which has been made toward achieving the eight goals. The reports made by this body in 1994 were very comprehensive and were complete.

This is the first time the legislative bodies of the U.S. Government have enacted an education reform law, and it is noteworthy that the Act was passed by a bipartisan vote. Maybe we have found a goal that both parties will support in the future as they have supported the passage of the Act. The goals to be achieved by the year 2000 are:

1. READY TO LEARN - All children will start to school ready to learn.

2. SCHOOL COMPLETION - Graduation rate will increase to at least 90%.

3. SCHOOL ACHIEVEMENT AND CITIZENSHIP Grades 4, 8, and 12 will be competent in English, mathematics, science, foreign languages, civics and government, economics, arts, history, and geography.

4. TEACHER EDUCATION AND PROFESSIONAL DEVELOPMENT - Teachers will have access to programs for the continued improvement of their professional skills and the opportunity to acquire the knowledge and skills needed to instruct and prepare all American students for the next century.

5. MATHEMATICS AND SCIENCE - U.S. students will be first in the world in mathematics and science achievement.

6. ADULT LITERACY AND LIFELONG LEARNING - Every adult American will be literate and will possess the knowledge and skills necessary to compete in a global economy and exercise the rights and responsibilities of citizenship.

7. SAFE, DISCIPLINED, AND ALCOHOL AND DRUG-FREE SCHOOLS - Every school in the United Sates will be free of drugs, violence, and firearms, and will offer a disciplined environment conducive to learning.

8. PARENTAL PARTICIPATION - Every school will promote partnerships that will increase parental involvement and participation in promoting the social, emotional, and academic growth of children.

All of these are very noble goals, and all of us would like for them to be achieved by the year 2000. However, probably none of them will be accomplished by the target date, if major changes are not made in our education systems.

The Federal Government has done a great job in setting national goals for all states to achieve. All who supported the passage of this Act should be commended, but accolades should be limited to the passage of incomplete legislation, because the Act does not finish the job. The Act does not finish the job because it does not require that standards, standard curriculum, and standard tests be established for each subject where improvement is necessary.

The Act leaves the preparation of standards, curricula development, and testing to each state. Should we believe that fifty states are going to produce fifty standards which will meet the needs of our nation in the coming generations of technical advances? Of course we should not. Why shouldn't we? The answer is a very simple one. Part of the problem we have in educating our children today has been caused by letting educators in each state determine what should be taught, how it should be taught, and how to measure achievement.

If we leave the job to each state, a good analogy is to picture fifty ant-covered logs (the logs being the states) floating down a river which leads to the sea. The ants (being state educators) are running around in circles and each one thinking it is steering. These logs will probably never reach shore before they are drifted out to sea.

We can't afford the mistake of again letting each state set the standards, write the curriculum for each subject, and prepare tests for measuring student learning. We have tried that, and know it won't work. Yes, we know about state's rights to educate their own. We also know that the states are not getting the job done.

Since the Federal Government is furnishing the money to each state to be used for improving education, the Federal Government should have the authority to produce standards, curriculum, and tests for each subject where improvement is required (that means practically all subjects). The standards, curriculum, and tests for each subject could be used as guides by the states. This was planned, but was met with opposition by many state educators and politicians. The authors think the standards, tests, and curricula should have been prepared over the protests of the states. We have to think about our country first, and this is no time to get into the State's Rights argument. If we do, our country will continue it's down-hill education slide.

Well, it's easy to say something won't work, but those who say the GOALS 2000 won't work should have a suggestion for something which will work. The authors who said GOALS 2000 won't work do have a plan which will work. That plan is to incorporate every, repeat every, suggested change which is recommended in this book. Making these changes will not be easy for several reasons. The education systems are so steeped in tradition that "educators" will resist any change. For example, we are still teaching Shakespeare and poetry writing to students who will have to go to work after high school, and we are not teaching what these students should know in order to get a job when they graduate. So much for this subject at this time.

Now that we have addressed what is wrong about GOALS 2000, let's address what is right about the Act.

Funding has been provided to help states improve education. This will quiet the ones who say we don't have enough money no matter what change is suggested. However, money is not the main ingredient which is needed. What is needed most is to get the so called educators and supervisors out of the traffic pattern and get good managers in their place. We must select school principles based on their ability to manage a school, maintain discipline, and motivate students and teachers. We should not select principals based on courses they have taken. The same applies to the selection process for school superintendents. Retired high ranking military personnel are well qualified to operate our schools. Let's get rid of the ones who have contributed to the downfall of education, and replace them with persons who can get our schools back to where they should be.

For 1995-96 approximately 400 million dollars have been allocated to support GOALS 2000. About 5% of the funds will be used by the Federal Government, 10% by the state education agencies, and the remainder, 85%, will go directly to the school districts and the schools in the form of subgrants. These subgrants will be awarded for three programs:

1. Professional development of personnel

2. Preservice training

3. Local reform

In order to qualify for these subgrants, schools must prepare a plan and have it approved before it will be funded. Maybe that will keep some districts from using the money to continue to staff their over-staffed organizations.

Progress reports will be issued annually to indicate how the nation and each state is doing toward the eight goals established by GOALS 2000. These reports are in a form so that even the most uneducated in reading graphs and reports can understand them. Just one look at these charts will tell anyone how we are doing toward meeting the goals which have been established. The charts are excellent.

Under Title V of the Act, a National Skills Standards Board has been established. The Board is to serve as a catalyst to stimulate the development and adoption of a voluntary national system of occupational skill standards and certification that will serve as a cornerstone of the strategy to enhance workforce skills. This Board, with the help of business and labor, will define the knowledge and skills needed for the complex, high-wage jobs of today and tomorrow. This is probably the best item which has come out of GOALS 2000, if schools will use the information which will be made available to them by the Board.

Some schools still think that their goal is to give their students a broad background of knowledge. This was true in medieval times, but is not true in today's world where specific knowledge is required. Most students will not go to college. Therefore, when these students graduate from high school they should be trained in a skill so they can get an entry level job in the workforce, and have enough academic knowledge to be able to be an asset to their company and to be able to advance in their skill. The National Skills Board will help the schools who establish technical/trade channels which will be recommended in this book.

Another board which should have been established would have been a board staffed by college educators and high school instructors. The mission of this board would be to bring high school graduates to the level where students could enter college with sufficient academic knowledge to pursue college level courses. It's time for us to get rid of remedial courses in our colleges.

Much good could have come from the Act, if standards and sample curricula and tests had been prepared for the states to use as a guide. Without such guidance, the states will probably continue to flounder around as they have done in the past. Higher standards, curricula, and tests are not the only things our schools need, but they are very necessary, if we are to accomplish the goals of GOALS 2000.

Mr. Riley, you are to be congratulated for having done a great job toward improving education. But, as I am sure you know, you stopped short of completing the job, because you didn't give those "ants on the logs" the directions for steering.

CHAPTER V

CRIME AND PUNISHMENT

If we do not control crime in our schools and in our nation, we cannot save our schools or our nation, and we are not even coming close to controlling crime. In fact, crime has increased dramatically since 1962 as reflected on the chart at the end of this chapter. Some of our citizens are afraid to walk on their streets during the day, and would not think of leaving their homes at night. Also, some of our students are afraid to go to school because of the crime being committed in school, and on the way to and from school. We have become prisoners in our own homes. We have burglar bars on our homes, because criminals are on the streets instead of in prison.

This situation began when the Supreme Court ruled out prayer in schools in 1962-63. At that time we saw the beginning of the:

1. Deterioration of the family.
2. Downhill slide in our education system.
3. Increase in the crime rate.

At or about the same time of the Supreme Court's ruling, judges in the 1960 era began to revolutionize the criminal justice system. Prior to that time, murder rates, venereal disease, robbery, and other crimes had been going down for decades. Two of the reasons why crime was on the decrease are; one, families stayed together and prayed together; and

63

two, punishment fit the crime. As soon as the justice system began to be overhauled, crimes began to increase, because "do-gooders" did not want the death sentence to be used. One of the 'do-gooders' is a justice who is now on the Supreme Court. This justice has been known to lament over the "poor criminal" who was being executed. Many people such as this Supreme Court justice want light sentences so criminals can be rehabilitated. They forget that you can't rehabilitate, if you haven't habilitated.

Over 90% of the criminals being incarcerated are dropouts from school. They came from poor and crime ridden areas, and they cannot support themselves except by crime. In most cases, it is too late in a criminal's life to rehabilitate. We must work on prevention, and the best preventative measure is education. A mandatory law is required so that all students must attend school until they are eighteen years old. Also, changes must be made to our education system so that every high school student will graduate with a skill which can be used to earn at least a living wage for himself. We also need to raise the standard for students who are preparing for college entry, so that colleges do not have to give remedial courses.

We can't do much to train all criminals so they can get a job when they are released from prison, but we can do more than we are doing. Criminals who have the ability and educational background to be trained should be segregated from hardened and untrainable criminals, and should be taught a skill before being released from prison. If necessary, their prison terms should be extended for the length of time it takes to train them. That's about all we can do for prisoners who are incarcerated, so we need to start taking preventative measures now.

Drugs and deadly weapons are associated with many criminal cases. Therefore, we need to solve the drug and deadly weapon problems. How do we do that? All we have to do is to do the same thing Singapore does - execute drug dealers and anyone who commits a crime while armed with a deadly weapon. Before Singapore gained their independence from England and Malaysia, that island country was the "sink hole of creation." Drugs and crime went hand in hand. Today it is a beautiful, prosperous, and almost crime free country. In fact, it is so prosperous that they have to import labor to meet all of the production contracts they have now, and expect to have in the future.

Many of our citizens will object to such "harsh and cruel" punishment, but the majority of our citizens would welcome laws which would eliminate drugs and crimes committed with a deadly weapon. They will welcome such laws because the criminals are committing "harsh and cruel" crimes. A person who becomes a drug addict may as well be dead - he is a loss to his family and a burden on society. Drug dealers have, for all intents and purposes, killed the victim. Therefore, the dealer should be executed.

Some will point out that children also deal in

drugs, and this is true, because they live in poverty, and in a crime ridden neighborhood, and have not been raised by a responsible family. How do we punish child drug dealers? We should punish them like a good father would punish them - he would tan their little bottoms so hard they wouldn't be able to sit down for a couple of days. Our justice system should do the same by publicly paddling them in front of their peers, and then sentencing them to go to school with the warning that they would get more of the same treatment, if they failed to go to school, behave themselves, and study. We wouldn't have to repeat this very many times before all of the other kids in the neighborhood would get out of the drug business. We should do the same for juvenile drug users. If anyone believes such punishment will not solve the problem, let's give it a try to prove them wrong.

A person who threatens with, or uses, a deadly weapon during the commission of a crime should be executed. If the criminal did not use the weapon, he would have if it had become necessary. Likewise, all accomplices to the crime should also be executed, even though they did not have in their possession, or use, a deadly weapon. Criminals must know that they will be executed, if they are a party to a crime where a deadly weapon was used, or possessed by anyone of the group during the commission of the crime. We wouldn't have to execute very many bur- glars, rapists, and other criminals before we would see a dramatic decrease in crime. Criminals must know that they will be given severe punishment, if they commit a crime.

Our prisons are overflowing with criminals, so a revolving door release policy has been devised. Over half of those released return to prison after committing another crime - sometimes killing or raping again. We should build enough prisons to keep prisoners long enough to serve their sentence. But building more prisons should not be our main goal. As was said before, we need to educate everyone. This will not eliminate crime, but it will minimize it.

Another criminal problem we must solve stems from our inability to control illegal immigration. Many of the illegals can't find work, so they commit crimes. These aliens overwhelm the courts, and contribute to the overflowing of our prisons. Here again, it is cheaper to stop illegal immigration than it is to house criminals. Also, illegal aliens who are not criminals become a burden, because we must educate and care for many of them and their children. We can't educate and care for all of our citizens as we should, so why do we strap ourselves to educate and care for illegal aliens?

In order to reduce our crime rate, we must make the punishment fit the crime - especially for murder and drug dealing. Some will say that a death sentence does not deter crime. The authors say - hog wash- and all of those who think the death sentence does not deter crime should go to Singapore and see for themselves that the death sentence does deter crime. If these "do-gooders" do not make a trip to Singapore to see for themselves that crime can be controlled by use of the death sentence, they should stop expounding their flawed theory.

The thing in life that any person fears the most is dying. Man spends all of his life consciously or unconsciously fearing death.

Therefore, we need to strengthen our laws so that the death sentence means a swift and timely death. Today a death sentence means that the criminal can continue for years to appeal his sentence even though he has been proven guilty. The appeal process costs are about $30,000 dollars a year for prison costs, and unknown court costs. Today there are about 3,000 criminals on death row, and we execute about 150 of them every year. At that rate, it will take 200 years to execute them. Our justice system has made a mockery of the death sentence.

A punishment for crime must be swift and fair. Parents do not spank their children tomorrow for a disobedience committed today. We must demand the death sentence for a crime in which a person is killed or could have been killed, and where a person deals in drugs. Also, we must demand longer sentences for other crimes, and we must keep criminals in prison until their sentences have been completed. The revolving door must have it's revolvers removed.

The second thing in life that a person fears most is loss of freedom. All of us want to be able to move about on this earth as we please. Therefore, we must strengthen our laws so that a criminal knows he will be incarcerated, and will be punished during his incarceration, if he is caught. We must stop building prisons which have all of the creature comforts of life - TV's, air-conditioning, telephones, fully equipped medical facilities, and gymnasiums, etc. Prisoners should not be better off than many of our law abiding citizens, and they should not be any better off than our military during wartime, or during training maneuvers. Most criminals should be housed in tents which would be located in the middle of a desert, or in frigid places such as Alaska. Those who commit crimes should know they are going to be severely punished while they are being incarcerated. Tent camps in undesirable places which would be run by retired drill sergeants should be the type of prison most of our criminals should be sent to. Let's quit coddling the hardened criminal.

Boot camps for some young , first time, criminals may turn some of them from a life of crime, if they are required to go back to school to learn a trade when they are released. Let's give this a try.

We can't change the composition of the family to what it was prior to WWII, but we can make families responsible for their children. Therefore, we need laws which will punish parents, if their children won't attend school, can't be controlled in school, or if their children commit a crime.

The juvenile laws we have today were designed to punish children who stole a pack of chewing gum, or a bicycle. They are not adequate for the crimes children commit today such as drug dealing and murder. Therefore, juvenile laws must be changed and punishment must fit the crime even though the person is a juvenile. Crime is at the root of many of the problems we have today, and we are hamstringing ourselves by not taking steps which are necessary to control crime. Unless we do, we cannot improve our school system and save our nation. Children cannot be educated, if they are not taught values at home and in the schools, and are afraid to walk to or from school. Teachers can't teach, if they are afraid of some of their students, and are afraid to walk to and from school. And, as has been said before, we cannot save our nation, if we cannot save our schools. And we can't save our schools if we can't control crime.

If anyone is against drastic punishment for criminals, that person is in the minority, is a part of the problem, and should step aside while the majority attempts to solve the problem.

In conclusion, we will never pass laws which require the stringent punishment recommended in this chapter, but let's hope we have the guts to pass laws which require punishment to fit the crime. For example, if a crime is committed where a deadly weapon is used in execution of the crime, the criminal should be executed, if a person is killed. If the gun was not used, the criminal should be sent to prison for the rest of his life. The prison he would spend the rest of his life in would be, for example, in Alaska where he will be cold all winter and suffer all summer from mosquitoes. If criminals know they will get at least a life sentence in tents in an undesirable climate if they use a gun, that will be all the gun law we will need. We must rid our society of persons who have killed, or would have killed another person. We shoot mad dogs, don't we? A person who would kill another person is comparable to a mad dog.

In summary, we don't need gun control laws, if we have laws which demand a death sentence for anyone who uses a gun during the commission of a crime. This is not a plug for the National Rifle Association. One of the authors contacted that organization and suggested that the association change their strategy from being against gun control laws to a strategy which advocates stiffer penalties for criminals who use a gun. The association did not respond.

Just one more paragraph on drugs. Our drug "war" is concentrated on the wrong end of the problem, because we can never stop the influx of drugs, just as we can't stop water from flowing down hill with a rake. We need to start on the other end of the problem - the dealers and the users. Of course, it is difficult to get to the king pin dealers, but it is fairly easy to get the in between dealers. They are standing on our streets every night dealing in drugs, and the police know who they are. If we were to execute a few of them, as we should, the rest of them would find some other occupation, and the king pins would have no one to sell their poison for them.

Drugs and poverty are the root causes for many of our crime problems. We can't get rid of poverty, but we can get rid of drug dealers, and anyone who uses a deadly weapon on another person.

WE CAN'T REHABILITATE MOST CRIMINALS, BUT WE CAN MAKE THE PUNISHMENT FIT THE CRIME. THEIR LIVING CONDITIONS WHILE IN PRISON SHOULD NOT BE BETTER THAN THE LIVING CONDITIONS OF OUR POOREST.

CHAPTER VI

CHARACTER EDUCATION

As we have seen, we are very far behind other countries when we compare the academic skills of out top students with the academic skills of top students from other nations. This, of course, is a major problem, but it can be solved by adopting all of the recommendations which will be presented in this book. However, there is another problem which will probably be the hardest to solve, but none of our problems can be solved until we find a way to solve this one. That problem is the moral decline of many of our people. We are now the world's most crime ridden nation in all of the industrialized world. Every day children are killing children for no good reason. This has resulted from the lack of character education in many of our homes and in our schools.

In Chapter III on the family, we learned that the conventional two-parent family, where the father supported the family by working and the mother cared for the children until they are able to live on their own, no longer exists for many families. In fact, the two-parent family where the mother is a full-time mother is now the exception. What difference does this make? It makes all the difference in the world. A child needs to be held closely by the mother the first years of the child's life. This closeness gives children confidence in the world into which they are born, programs the brain to love and be loved, and instills the desire to be like thier parents.

The next year, the "terrible twos", is also a very important year in the child's life. During this period, the child learns that the parent's authority is absolute, and that the parent must be obeyed. Then from that time on, the parents continue to teach morality, and the difference between right and wrong. In Christian/Judeo families, the Ten Commandments and the Golden Rule were used as a teaching tool. Other families who did not use the Ten Commandments, used the essence of these laws to teach their children the difference between right and wrong. Also, the public schools taught the Ten Commandments and the Golden Rule as they had done since the very beginning of this country.

Teaching the Ten Commandments in public schools was prohibited by the Supreme Court who misinterpreted the First Amendment to the Constitution of the United States. That Amendment prohibited the Congress from passing a law establishing a State church and passing a law prohibiting the free exercise of religion. The nine old men on the Court at that time interpreted the Amendment to require the "separation of church and state" which is not what the Amendment says - it's only the interpretation of the Supreme Court. Since their interpretation is so far from what the Amendment says it can be assumed that they had trouble understanding plain English. It can also be assumed that they did not refer to, or read, the many volumes written by the authors of the Constitution in which their thoughts concerning prayer in schools are expressed. As a result of the Court's ruling, many of our citizens have been brainwashed into believing the Supreme Court's interpretation. Read the Amendment yourself to determine whether it says "separation of church and state", or even implies it. It only says that Congress cannot pass a law establishing a state church. It also gives a mandate that Congress cannot pass a law prohibiting the free exercise of religion. By the 1962 ruling of the Court, the free exercise of religion was abolished by prohibiting prayer in public schools. This must change, and will be changed, we hope, in the near future.

At the same time the Supreme Court ruled out prayer in the public schools, religious and moral training in the home began to deteriorate. Two working parents, and single parent families did not have time to teach their children how to have self-respect, respect for others, and the difference between right and wrong. In some families the parents did not have adequate moral training themselves. What do we do about the problem? There is only one answer - we must start moral training in all schools from kindergarten through the entire formal education of our students, including college.

The authors can hear the backlash from teachers who already have more to teach than they can. It's true that teachers are having a hard time teaching all that should be taught to their students. But some of the teaching time is taken up with trying to motivate uncaring students and fighting off the more aggressive ones. If we had a good moral training program in our public schools and in our homes, we could change some of the behavior problems teachers must contend with. This has been proven in many schools that have found it necessary to hire principals who are disciplinarians, and to make moral training a part of their curricula. These principals have also demanded responsibility from the parents for education of their children.

How do we get moral training into the classroom when many of our teachers are not qualified to teach this subject? We start by including moral training in colleges where teachers are trained. But we can't wait for the pipeline to turn out teachers who know how to teach morality to their students, and we don't have to. There is a nonprofit organization which has prepared training programs for all grades from kindergarten through the eighth grade. Their program has been approved in all fifty states, and is being used in over 50,000 classrooms today, with great success.

The work the company has done has eliminated the need for each district to prepare a course of instruction for each grade level. Their courses come complete with lesson plans, posters, reproducibles, and help for the home room teacher to successfully conduct a moral training program during the time which is ordinarily wasted. It has been found that students are very receptive to the program. This acceptance by the students proves that students want to learn not only subject matter but how to conduct themselves and live their lives. This program is the best thing that has come down the pike since the wrongful ruling of the Supreme Court.

This program is available to every school district that wishes to purchase the program for each of their teachers. The cost is about $95.00 for each teacher in each grade level, and the material is reusable for many years. Some districts will complain that they can't afford the program. The authors think they cannot afford to not buy the program. Some districts have found that local businesses will contribute some money for the program, if the district can't afford the entire cost. It is recommended that each school district explore the use of the program and opt to use it. If they do, it is strongly recommended that a classroom teacher - not a counselor or some other staff person - be relieved of their classroom duties and be given the responsibility for implementing the program in the district. If this is not done, the program may fail, and has failed in some districts because the program was not properly implemented and followed-up.

The company which developed this program is:
Character Education Institute
8918 Tesoro, Suite 575
San Antonio, TX 78217-6253
Telephone # 800-284-0499
Contact: Dr. Mulkey, Ph.D.

Implementing this program should be one of the first changes any district should make. It's affordable, very easily incorporated, and results can be measured almost immediately.

CHARACTER EDUCATION MUST BECOME THE RESPONSIBILITY OF OUR SCHOOLS, BECAUSE IT IS NOT BEING DONE IN MANY OF OUR HOMES, AND CHARACTER DEVELOPMENT IS A PART OF THE EDUCATION PROCESS.

A GOOD AND CHEERFUL ATTITUDE IS PROBABLY THE MOST IMPORTANT ASSET MOST EMPLOYERS LOOK FOR IN A NEW OR PROSPECTIVE EMPLOYEE. A PERSON WHO HAS A GOOD ATTITUDE WILL SUCCEED IN THIS WORLD, IF THE GOOD ATTITUDE IS BACKED-UP BY GOOD CHARACTER. WE MUST TEACH THE VALUE OF A GOOD ATTITUDE DURING CHARACTER EDUCATION.

CHAPTER VII

UNIFORMS / PEER PRESSURE / SEX

Now that our schools are teaching values let's try introducing another change which will improve our educational system. This change will not only improve our teaching, it will reinforce the value training which we have started to teach in our classrooms. We won't have to teach in order to reap the benefits of this change. All we have to do is make the change.

This change is having students wear uniforms to school. Such a change will be resisted by almost everyone, including some students, some parents, the American Civil Liberties Union (ACLU), and probably by the Courts. Some, especially the Civil Liberties Union, will say that requiring students to wear uniforms violates the Constitution as the Constitution would probably be interpreted by that organization. That organization probably would like to attack the military for requiring the wearing of a uniform, but they know they would lose that one. They can be made to lose the wearing of uniforms in public schools issue, if the Courts are given strong reasons for the requirement to wear uniforms. Some parents will also object, because they want their children to be able to "express themselves" by the clothes they wear. Other parents will object, because buying uniforms will be more than they can afford. This may be true to some extent, but if it is true, school districts should consider increasing their budgets so they can partially subsidize the purchase of uniforms for their students. Most parents will want their children to wear uniforms, if they are told about the advantages of having students wear uniforms.

Why do we need to require the wearing of uniforms? If all students are required to wear uniforms, we would have fewer students joining gangs. Many students join gangs because they want to be a part of a group, and want to have recognition from the group, and from others outside the group. Wearing uniforms will satisfy the desire of many of our students who want to "belong". Once uniforms have been adopted by a school, pride in wearing the uniform of their school can be instilled in the students. This pride will translate into more self-confidence and higher self-esteem.

Another reason for wearing uniforms is to reduce peer pressure as much as possible. Peer pressure is one of the most difficult problems which are experienced by students - especially those who cannot afford to wear the same clothes that the wealthier students wear. If all students wear uniforms, the playing field is leveled to some extent. This will help the wealthier students by teaching them that they are no better than the poorest. It will also help the poorer students by ridding them of the "inferiority" they feel, because they cannot wear name-brand jeans and $150.00 athletic shoes. The atmosphere in the classroom will be more conducive to learning, if all students are "leveled" by wearing uniforms.

Still another benefit is the elimination of "sexy" clothing being worn in the classroom. This is especially necessary when the children reach the age of puberty. At that age, students are confused, bewildered, excited, inquisitive, happy, and don't know what to do about their newly-found ability to create in their own image. That is the time when we need to eliminate sexy clothes so that students can concentrate on learning instead of concentrating on the girl or boy in the next seat.

When students reach puberty, it is the time to separate the sexes in the classrooms. Students at that time in their lives need to be able to concentrate on learning, not on sex. The wearing of uniforms will minimize this problem by eliminating short skirts, tight jeans, and short shorts for girls, and tight jeans, short shorts, muscle shirts, and unbuttoned shirts for boys. In short, uniforms will eliminate the advertising of their physical assets. Last, but not least, the wearing of uniforms will eliminate gang members from wearing clothes to school which identify them as being members of a gang. This practice can be eliminated by the school administrators, if they have enough "guts" to do it. Everyone including teachers, administrators, and the police know what clothes are worn by the gangs. District officials have the authority to specify what clothes can and cannot be worn by students. If we can't sell uniforms right away, let's concentrate on eliminating gang and sexy clothes in schools.

In addition to requiring the wearing of uniforms, each school should have a school song. It doesn't have to be a musical great, but it must be spirited and easily sung. The music of any of the college school songs, or of military marching songs could be used. The song should be memorized by all students, and should be sung at pep rallies, games, and any time the school body is assembled.

If a school adopts wearing a uniform, teaches values, and has school spirit as evidenced by the singing of "their song", that school will see a reduction in dropouts, an improvement in grades, and teachers will be proud they are teaching at that school. With all the benefits that the wearing of a uniform will bring to a school, why not get started now? It will be the best thing a school district can do to help solve some of the problems which the district has.

In closing this chapter, for those who doubt the benefits which would accrue, let's suggest that they go to a parochial or private school where uniforms are worn. There they can get a first hand opinion concerning the wearing of uniforms, if they talk to the faculty and observe the conduct of the students. What they will find will convince even the most skeptical.

WEARING UNIFORMS TO SCHOOL WILL IMPROVE THE ATTITUDE OF STUDENTS, AND AN IMPROVEMENT IN ATTITUDE WILL RESULT IN BETTER LEARNING.

CHAPTER VIII

YEAR-ROUND SCHOOL

In earlier chapters we addressed the need for character education and elimination of peer pressure. As has been said before, we can't make changes in series, because there is so much to be done that half of a century would pass before we would get all of the changes made. The world will pass us by, if we delay making the changes. Therefore, we must make as many changes as we can in parallel. Now let's consider a change that doesn't cost any more money and one which can be easily implemented in parallel with other changes. This change is not only easily implemented, but positive results can be seen almost as soon as the program is started. We won't have to wait for a long time to see whether our change will bear fruit. The change which can be implemented immediately by any school board is to change from nine month school to year-round school.

We said the change won't cost any more money. We should have said it won't cost any more money than the district now has. Of course, year-round school will require secretarial and janitorial services and utilities during the summer months. Where can the district get the money for services that will be required during the summer? In many school districts, overhead has grown at a very rapid rate in recent years, and the rate at which it has grown is about the same as the rate at which school funding has increased. As more funds have become available to some districts, salaries for superintendents, etc., and the number of assistants have increased to where the overhead is as high as 50% in some school districts. That is unreal. Too much of the funds which have become available have been used to support employees who contribute little or nothing to instruction in the classrooms. This must be changed. It's no wonder we can't pay good teachers what they are worth.

Before districts begin a year-round program, they should estimate the additional costs, and eliminate enough overhead to pay for the added costs. Reducing the overhead is going to require that districts operate with less secretarial help and educator staff such as assistants to assistant principals, assistants to assistant superintendents, and many other overhead personnel found in many school districts. Such a reduction will not hurt instruction. In fact, it will help because there will be fewer people asking for reports, etc., from the teacher level, and will get instruction back where it belongs - in the classroom. If, after implementation of year-round school and cutting overhead, the district thinks it needs help in curricula development, etc., it can ask for help from the classroom teachers. They'll be happy to help, and will probably do a better job than the so called "education specialists".

Before we go any further, we need to recall why we have school only nine months a year. This practice began when we first started public schools in the United States. Then we were an agrarian society, and the farmers needed their children to help with the crops during the summer. Today less than 2% of our population live on farms. Nine month schools are like many other school policies and teachings that are outdated but continue because "that is the way we always did it."

Year-round schools have many advantages. Some, but not all of them, are listed below:

1. We won't have to build as many schools in the future as we have in the past because one-fourth of the students will not be in school at any one time. This will be a saving to the tax payers.

2. Teacher "burnout" will be eliminated, or at least alleviated, because teachers will be given a break before they start to "climb the walls".

3. Students will retain an interest in the subjects being taught if they know they will be given a break before they too "begin to climb the walls".

4. Students will retain more after a short break period than they would after a three-month vacation.

5. The dropout rate will be reduced, because the students will be given a short break before they lose interest.

6. School vandalism will be reduced, because the buildings will always be occupied.

7. Students will be more motivated to learn when

they know the learning period will be followed by a break period.

8. Only one-fourth of the students will be on the streets at any time, so teenage crime will be reduced.

9. Temporary jobs for students will be easier to find since the demand will be less with only one-fourth of the students looking for jobs.

10. Businesses can count on teenage help being available all year.

11. Students who are behind in their school work will have a chance to catch up during the break period.

12. The number of school days can be increased above the traditional 180.

Year-round school is not something new. It is being adopted by more schools every year. At this writing, there are over 800 schools which are operating year-round programs.

What is the difference between nine month and year-round schools? Nine month schools have a three month vacation period after nine months of school. Year-round schools have classes twelve months of the year, but only three-fourths of the students are in school at any one time. The other fourth is on a break period. After a designated time, one-fourth of the students attending class go on break and the fourth that has been on break go back to school.

There are a number of combinations that can be used. One is for the students to attend class for six weeks, and then go on break for two weeks (in class for 30 school days and on break for 10 school days). This plan will probably be found to be one of the best, because it will probably be more easily adapted to the teaching units now being used in many schools.

Another plan is for students to attend school for nine weeks, and be on break for three weeks (in class for 45 school days and on break for 15 school days). Other plans are 60-20, 75-25, and 90-30. All are workable, and all have many advantages over the conventional nine month school.

The year-round systems are being implemented for the benefit of the students, but as we have seen, many more benefits are derived. As we know, students, just as we, have an interest retention span problem. If we can't see the light at the end of the tunnel, we begin to lose interest. And, when students begin to lose interest, they stop learning. When learning stops, students become disruptive, and discipline problems start. Interest in any academic subject is hard to retain for a nine months period. Also, it has been found that a continuity of learning is enhanced when short breaks are given often.

Teachers find it hard to motivate for a period as long as nine months, and they begin to lose interest in teaching. Before the nine months are over they are ready to throw in the towel. Shorter teaching periods will solve this problem.

Another benefit is that students who are behind in their school work will have an opportunity to get up to speed if they are tutored during a break period. Some teachers would be willing to become tutors during their break period for a small stipend. Of course, this would require the cutting of more overhead.

Now we have found a way to improve our school system - one that doesn't cost any more money, one which can be implemented, and one which even the most "dyed in the wool" educators can find little, if any, fault.

All of us can help in this effort - teachers, parents, PTA organizations, lay persons, and school board members. So, let's all get behind this effort so we can chalk up another victory in the war for education reform.

Once we have the year-round plan implemented, and positive results have been shown, we will have the confidence of the school board. This will help us when we try to make other changes.

Now let's prepare ourselves for the next change we can make. We say let's prepare ourselves because this one may cost more money than the district may have. Any change requiring more money is going to be a "hard sell". But, sell after school activities until 5:00 PM we must because it solves so many problems. So, turn to the next chapter and let's get started with after school activities.

However, before we start on the next chapter, we

need to point out one mistake that some districts have made when they implemented year-round school. They did not implement the program entirely in the school. They let parents and teachers decide which program they wanted to be a part of. Once the district plans to implement year-round school in middle school X, implementation should be complete for school X. It is a mistake to try to have two separate programs in one school.

CHAPTER IX

AFTER SCHOOL ACTIVITIES

Now that we have installed year-round school, have started teaching values, and our students are wearing uniforms, let's take one more step that will improve our schools. However, this step may cost more money than the school board can save by reducing overhead. The change is to have after school activities until the students' parents arrive home from work.

We said, after school activities may cost more than the district has available. Just as we paid for utilities, janitorial services, and administrative costs in order to have year-round school we can probably do some more cutting of overhead in order to have after school activities.

Every state and every school district has overhead personnel that can be eliminated or put to work in the after school activities. The elimination of wasteful overhead will not only help finance after school activities, it will do two other things; one, it will reduce the paper work which classroom teachers must do in order to satisfy overhead people who generate requirements for reports so they can justify their jobs; two, it will reduce the number of personnel who are between the classroom instructor and the school superintendent. As we make changes in our schools, reducing the number of overhead jobs should always be one of our goals. We need to give classroom teachers more authority, and control over their teaching.

Why will after school activities cost more? Again, we will need more utilities and clerical help, but the thing we will need the most are personnel who can supervise the after school activities. Teachers have done their duty by teaching all day and should not be asked to do duty after school. In place of teachers, we can hire retired military who have had supervisory experience during most of their military career, and are well-qualified in maintaining discipline. These retired personnel can be teachers or teacher aids. They can be used to maintain discipline in the school, and can do a great job of handling after school activities. Now that we have solved at least part of the money and personnel problems, let's determine which students will participate in after school activities. All students should be required to attend, if they do not have a valid reason for not attending. By a valid reason, we mean the parents should come to the school, and justify why their child should not attend the after school program. Those who should not be excused are latchkey students, and students who are failing. The failing students should be provided with a motivated teacher and a study facility. There will be teachers who will teach after school provided they are paid for their services. Also, many retired military are capable of teaching many of the subjects, and all are capable of motivating failing students.

After school activities should be provided for students who want to learn more about the subjects they are studying in school. They should be given advanced courses. Other students may want to study subjects which are not taught in the classroom, or they may want to do hobby work. These students should be accommodated with a hobby shop, or with courses in aviation, astronomy, medicine, or any other course for which there is an interest.

Now that we have established after school activities, let's see what we have accomplished, or are in the process of accomplishing.

1. We have kept students off the street until their parents come home from work. This is probably the best result, because children should not be at home and unsupervised. If they are left to their own devises, they will probably get into trouble in one way or another. Some will get pregnant or in trouble with the law. Juveniles must not be allowed to go unsupervised at home or in any other place.

2. Slow learners will be helped to the extent that we may be able to motivate them, or to overcome some learning disability. If we are successful with slow learners or unmotivated students we can keep them in school until they are graduated. Ninety percent of inmates are dropouts. We must plug this hole, and it can be plugged, to some extent, with after school activities. We cannot afford to have "throwaway" people. It costs too much to build jails for them, or to support them on welfare.

3. After school activities will accommodate the gifted by giving them challenging courses. The

gifted are the ones we need to send to college, so they can become leaders in industry and government.

4. Some students become bored with the "nuts and bolts" that must be taught in public school. During after school classes we can take time to demonstrate applications of mathematics, physics, and writing, etc. More will be covered in applying what is being taught in other chapters, but for the time being, we can start applying what is being taught during after school activities, so that students can see a need for the subjects in the real world.

5. We have given the students the opportunity to study the subjects that they have an interest in. Many students will look forward to the end of the academic day so they can study the subjects they want to study. This will be a carrot for them.

6. Some students just want to play after school. For these students, we will give them the opportunity to participate in intramural sports, or to just shoot baskets. Either way the sports will be supervised, and will provide an opportunity to teach values and cooperation, etc.

The benefits of after school activities cannot be over emphasized. Therefore, we need to start the program now - not sometime in the distant future. It can be done now. We probably have the funds, if we reduce the wasteful overhead by eliminating jobs or assigning some overhead personnel to after school activities. One school district reduced their overhead, and saved 1.9 million dollars, so don't say it can't be done. Also, we have the personnel in the form of retired military. They are well-qualified for many school jobs, and they don't require much training in the education field. They have been teaching during most of their career. Let's use their talents.

AFTER SCHOOL ACTIVITIES IS NOT A BABY SITTING PROGRAM. IT IS A PROGRAM TO TEACH OUR STUDENTS AS MUCH AS POSSIBLE BEFORE RETURNING THEM TO THEIR PARENTS.

CHAPTER X

COMPULSORY EDUCATION

In Chapter I we justified the need for educating everyone. As a review, we stated that only a small number of unskilled jobs will be available in the future, and, that even now, the average job requires two years of education beyond high school. Technology is developing at such a rapid rate that there will be no work for the uneducated in the near future. If there are any U.S. jobs which can be performed by the uneducated, they will be exported to a country where labor rates are lower than in the United States.

What must we do about this problem? We must educate everyone. How do we accomplish this seemingly impossible task? It won't be easy, but it must be done. The following are some of the things which must be done before we can even hope to educate everyone:

We must have a federal law, or each state must pass a mandatory education law, which will require that students must stay in school until they are eighteen years old, or have graduated from high school. A federal law will be almost impossible to obtain, because the federal government does not have that much control over education. The Department of Education can suggest that every state pass such a law, and can threaten the withholding of federal funds to states which do not have such a law, but that is about all the Feds can do. This leaves the problem to the states. Why do we need such a law?

We need such a law so that students can be required to stay in school until they can be taught enough so they can get a job when they graduate. This will help reduce crime, because the law will keep juveniles off the streets, and out of Satan's workshop. About 90% of our criminals are dropouts. If we force students to stay in school until they are at least 18 years old or have graduated from high school, we can teach them enough for them to make a living when they graduate. It won't be much of a living, because, as we have said before, the average job now requires about two years of training beyond high school.

If GOALS 2000 is adopted by all states, a mandatory law requiring school attendance until eighteen years old will be a necessity, if we are going to even approach some of the goals which have been established by GOALS 2000. For example, to achieve a high school graduation rate of 90% by the year 2000 can only be achieved by requiring all students to attend school until they are eighteen years old.

However, before, repeat before, we pass such a law, we must change the curricula beginning at the sixth grade. Why must we make such curricula changes? Many of our students are not capable of, or have no desire for continuing in the academic channel. Also, many of them cannot see the relevance of Shakespeare, mathematics beyond simple arithmetic, history, music, etc., to finding a job when they graduate. However, many of our students are capable of, and have an interest in, studying subjects such as electronics, machinery, aircraft, business, health, and other job related subjects. We don't have to send all students to college. The world needs skills to perform technician duties. Therefore, we must, beginning at the sixth grade, start channeling students into academic and technical/trade channels. This subject is covered in more detail in Chapter XIII "Curricula."

Studies have shown that the jobs of the immediate future will require at least two years of education beyond high school. One goal should be that most of our college students will graduate with a professional degree that is in demand such as; science, engineering, mathematics, computer science, business, and marketing. These are the professions which are necessary for the United States to be able to compete with the rest of the world in manufacturing, scientific advances, medicine, services, and world trade.

Not all students will be able to go to college and graduate with professional degrees which will be in demand. Therefore, another goal must be that we establish public training programs for students who cannot, or don't want to, become professionals. These courses should be designed to train a student to be able to perform as a technician, or skilled worker in the many jobs which do not require a degree, but do require a high degree of skill or knowledge. Many companies which have a need for engineers also have a need for technicians. In fact, some of these companies have to hire engineers to perform technician duties, because technicians are not available. The same is true for skills in automotive, aircraft, medicine, business, computer, and other fields where technical knowledge or a skill will be sufficient.

Let's get our youth off the streets, and into class-rooms. If we do, and make the suggested curricula changes which have been presented, we will have a chance to educate everyone. And, educate everyone, we must.

WE CAN'T EDUCATE OUR YOUTH IF WE CAN'T GET THEM OFF THE STREETS AND INTO THE CLASSROOMS.

CHAPTER XI

MINORITIES AND ATHLETES

Not one of us had the choice of whether to be born or not to be born. Neither did we have a choice of what race we were to be born into. Therefore, we must do the best we can with our lot whether it be African American, American Indian, Alaskan Indian, Asian, Caucasian, Native Hawaiian, Mexican American, or some other race. Also, we do not know why we were born. We only know we can make a difference in this world, if we apply ourselves. We can make this space ship a better place on which to live. We must all pull together, because it will take all of us to make our country great again. All of us would like to improve our situation, and would like to give our children a better future than we had. The only way we can do this is to better educate ourselves and our children. Let's put this in capital letters in order to help us remember it. THE ONLY WAY WE CAN HELP OURSELVES AND OUR CHILDREN IS BY EDUCATING OURSELVES AND OUR CHILDREN. How to better educate ourselves and our children is what this book is about.

Family income and education level of parents is directly proportional to the Scholastic Achievement Test (SAT) scores which will be made by students. Since low income and low education level of parents is a major problem affecting minorities, let's take time to examine the charts which reflect this relationship.

ANNUAL FAMILY INCOME	SAT SCORE
Less than $10,000	768
$10,000 to $20,000	813
$20,000 to $30,000	857
$30,000 to $40,000	887
$40,000 to $50,000	900
$50,000 to $60,000	933
$60,000 to $70,000	953
Over $70,000	1025

PARENTS EDUCATION LEVEL	SAT SCORE
No High School	768
High School Graduate	840
Associate Degree	865
Bachelor Degree	947
Graduate Degree	1012

From these charts we can see that family income and parent education level are factors we must address when trying to find ways to better educate everyone, especially our minorities, because many of them fall into the category of poor and under educated.

The United States is now predominately white Caucasian English speaking people, but the ratio of Anglos to ethnic groups will change. In fact, by the year 2050 Anglos will be only 52.5% of the population. Hispanics and African Americans are the fastest growing minorities and will comprise much of the balance of 47.5% of the population in the United States. We must take action now to better educate all minorities, if we want to prevent a crisis between now and mid-century.

Presently about 25% of our population lives below the poverty level, although many of them work at the best job they can find - usually a laboring job. These kinds of jobs are fast disappearing, and by mid-century there will be practically no laboring jobs. There will be some unskilled jobs such as in fast food restaurants, but they will not pay enough for a family to live on. If we do not take action now to educate all Americans, the proportion of hungry and uneducated in our country will rise as the population grows.

Although the minorities will be approximately one-half of our population by mid-century, business and social life will continue to be very much as it is today. Therefore, minorities and Anglos should educate and prepare themselves to fit into mainstream America. This is not accepted by some minorities who would like to continue living the way they do today. This is especially true of Native Indians, many Mexican Americans, and many African Americans. Therein lies one of the problems in trying to educate them. From their actions, it could be assumed they value their heritage more than they value their future, and the future of the United States. Such an assumption would cause some minorities to become angry, and some who have read this book so far, will stop reading. So be it, but these groups must face the facts. They must overcome the disadvantages that minorities in America are faced with, if they are going to succeed. Minorities must remember that the only ones who can stop them from succeeding is they themselves. Getting ahead in this world is not easy for anyone, especially for minorities. Let's all admit this fact and get on with our lives.

General Colin Powell was asked how he handled discrimination. His answer was - if anyone wants to discriminate against me, let them. It won't bother me because I'll be too busy making myself to be as good as, or better than, the discriminators. There is your answer to how to handle discrimination. Just get yourself busy trying to be as good as, or better than, anyone else at your job or profession.

African Americans will have the most difficulty in getting ahead, and they cannot get ahead, if they don't educate themselves. Government has done as much as it can to give African Americans a chance to succeed. We can't legislate the end of discrimination. In our lifetime, we will not see the end of discrimination. Education is the only way blacks can hope to ever alleviate the problem. If blacks educate themselves, they can get better jobs and will be able to better their living conditions. Blacks who educate themselves will be more acceptable to

Anglos, but some discrimination will still be there. They will never be accepted by all whites, and this problem is one they will have to live with all of their lives. The time has not come when Dr. King's vision, that all men will be judged by their character rather than by the color of their skin, will not come in our life time. Sad, but true.

Many African Americans blame the country for their problems, because their ancestors were slaves. This fact does play a part, but it must not dominate. Many races have been slaves including Jews who were slaves during a large part of their history, and they overcame. African Americans can overcome, if they will put their past in the past, and get on with educating themselves. African Americans should be thankful that they don't have to try to get ahead in Africa where opportunities are almost nil, and where a slave can be bought today for about $30.00.

Another problem African Americans have in being accepted is caused by the way they live and conduct themselves. We are referring to their mannerisms which most Anglos are not willing to have brought into the workplace and into the schools. This coupled with the way many African Americans speak English creates more acceptability problems. These problems can be overcome, if a person is willing. Blacks should think this over, and should try to remember that many blacks have succeeded, and have become prominent. How did they do this? They educated themselves. Blacks should ask themselves whether they are willing to put past slavery and discrimination aside, and begin preparing themselves for the future. If the answer is yes, they must remember that no one can stop them except themselves. Of course, it's a hard row to hoe, but it must be hoed.

Poverty makes the problems worse, and no one has found a solution for the poverty problem which affect all Americans. In fact, the poor are getting poorer. Some blacks will let this stop them, but others won't. We will offer a solution for some blacks in one of the following paragraphs.

Some of the black's problems could be alleviated, if some black organization would start a crusade to tell blacks the facts of life, and show them a way to a better education, and a better way of life. The NAACP is no longer a useful organization in the struggle to make life better for blacks. That organization wants to concentrate on quotas, more legislation, and enforcement of civil rights laws. We can't legislate more for blacks, and quotas would take away some of the free enterprise which we all cherish. If the NAACP would concentrate on programs to better educate, and how to make blacks more acceptable to Anglos, they would be doing a great service. How about it NAACP? Are you willing and able to do what must be done to improve the lot of African Americans? The Black Caucus in the House of Representatives could help, if they would. All blacks should write to their congressman to ask for their help, and should send a copy to the members of the Black Caucus and the NAACP.

Now let's address the problems the Mexican Americans have in trying to make a better life for themselves and for their children. The problems of many Mexican Americans can be summed up in one assumption which is, that they are more concerned with their heritage than they are concerned with their future. Let's put that in capital letters, IT CAN BE ASSUMED THAT THEY ARE MORE CONCERNED WITH THEIR HERITAGE THAN THEY ARE CONCERNED WITH THEIR FUTURE. What justifies such an assumption? Many things do, but let's start with language. Many Mexican Americans speak Spanish in their homes, and when they converse with each other. What problems does this cause? Let's list them.

1. Many of their children come to school with a very limited knowledge of English, or are unable to speak English. These children come to school with two strikes on them. They find themselves in a place which is foreign to them. They are anything but motivated to learn, and they are scared and want to go home. Mexican American families are tying one hand behind their children's backs by speaking Spanish in their homes. Their children will probably live with this handicap the rest of their lives.

2. Spanish as the first language in the home limits the vocabulary of their children. It's hard enough to acquire a good vocabulary in any language, especially in English. Asking anyone to be proficient in two languages is ask-

ing something that most of us can't do, so why burden a child with this problem?

3. Our ears, vocal cords, and facial and tongue muscles are trained to communicate in one language. If we try to master two languages, we will probably speak with an accent in one of the languages. Whether we like it or not, if job seekers speak English with an accent, they will have one strike against them no matter how qualified they may be. For some jobs which require oral communication, they will have three strikes before they complete the interview.

Many Mexican Americans live in poverty. Some will let this condition be their excuse for not trying to get a better education. Some will not. Many successful Mexican Americans came from poverty plagued homes. We will offer a plan for the very bright Mexican Americans in a later paragraph, and we wish we had a solution for all who live in poverty. We don't, and no one else does either, but we know that education can get individuals out of poverty.

Many of the problems that Mexican Americans are faced with are self-inflicted. Most Mexican American organizations devote their time and energy to promoting the Mexican way of life. Mexican Americans need an organization which will tell them the facts of life. The facts are that many will live in poverty the rest of their lives, and so will their children, if they continue to be more concerned with their heritage than with becoming mainstream Americans. The Mexican American Caucus in the House of Representatives could be a moving force to change priorities, if they would. The future of Mexican Americans and the future of this country is at stake. Look at the education level of Mexican Americans in the following chart. Only African Americans score less on the SAT than they do.

1995 SAT SCORES

Asian Americans	956
White Americans	946
American and Alaskan Indians	850
Mexican Americans	802
African Americans	744
Average	859

Let's compare the 1995 average score with the average score before 1962 which at that time had been averaging about 971. This tells us how far our education level has dropped. Don't you think it's about time that we overhaul our education system, and start educating all of us better than we have since 1962? All students including Anglos and minorities are scoring less than students scored before 1962.

Ethnic groups, except Asian Americans, will need the most help in order to better educate them. Therefore, we must do all we can to educate our minorities. We must do this in order to reduce the number of minorities on relief rolls and in prison, and to keep the number from rising as the population of our ethnic groups grow. Also, we must do it, if we are going to compete economically with the rest of the world. We need an educated population-not welfare recipients and prison inmates.

Before 1962 SAT scores averaged about 971. Since Anglos in 1995 scored only 946, over 30 points below 1962 scores, we must find a way to better educate some of them also. However, our primary goal should be to raise the standard of the Mexican Americans and the African Americans so that their scores are equal to Anglo scores. We must educate all of our citizens, if we are to be able to compete. Persons on welfare and in prisons are anchors in our society. If we educate the welfare recipients, they will be a part of the force that drives our country - not anchors.

Having said, many times, that we must educate everyone, let's address how we are going to accomplish this task.

AMERICAN AND ALASKAN INDIANS AND ESKIMOS

These groups of students and people are cared for by the Bureau of Indian Affairs. About all we can do for these minorities is to wish them better luck with the Bureau in the future than they have had in the past.

AFRICAN AMERICANS

In 1995 blacks scored lower than any other minority group on the SAT, and they are one of the fastest growing segments of our population. Therefore, this is the group which should receive the highest priority. How do we go about doing this? First, we must motivate them to help themselves. Therein lies the problem, because many come to school not motivated to learn. We can point out that they can go as high as they want to, if they will make the effort. We can also point out that black professionals do not suffer the discrimination that most blacks do. Ask any Anglo professional how he feels about a black counterpart, and he'll tell you he has the utmost respect for everyone who educates himself, and behaves like a professional. The key to minimizing discrimination is education and conduct. Therefore, on their way to the top, blacks must be able to handle the discrimination they will receive. Once they get to the top, much of the discrimination they felt will be considerably less. It won't disappear, but it will be tolerable, especially when they have a job which gives them financial security.

General Powell has given blacks this advice "Young people, you must prepare yourselves - you must be ready because there will be opportunities, if you are prepared. Conversely, there will not be opportunities, if you are not prepared. Opportunities exist not only in the military, but also in every endeavor in life." General Powell is only one of many blacks who have achieved their goals in life. Blacks should make a list of blacks who have made names for themselves. There are many, but not one of them did so without an education.

Some blacks, especially university students, want

to wear so called African dress, want to keep themselves out of mainstream America, and want to concentrate their studies on African history, etc., and some universities encourage this. Studying African history is good to some extent, but their main effort should be to study the history of the United States to learn how this country became great. They will learn that all of us were minorities at one time, and that all of us put our shoulders to the wheel in order to make this country great. We need the African Americans to put their shoulders to the wheel now in order to make this country great again.

Poverty is probably the main barrier to educating the blacks, so we must do all we can to remove this barrier for all blacks, especially the ones who are qualified for higher education, and who are held back by poverty. We should physically remove them from their environment, and place them in a boarding school along with Anglos who are being held back by poverty. Of course, this will cost money, but it won't cost as much as supporting them on welfare or in prisons later in life. We hope that such a program will be funded. It will not only help some blacks, it will help many other black students, because it will give them a goal for which to aim.

Another way we may try to educate more blacks would be to bus many of them to predominately white schools. In many areas, we are more segregated than we were before the Civil Rights Movement. Children learn from each other. Black students, if mixed with Anglo students, would soon speak like the Anglos, and would begin to lose their mannerisms which they acquired while in predominately back schools.

Another way to help the blacks would be for more blacks who have succeeded in life to take a day off each month, and speak before black student bodies. They could inspire some of the students to work harder at educating themselves.

We can't continue to class many blacks as "throwaway people." We need them in the work force, but they must be educated in order to fit into this highly technical world in which we are living.

MEXICAN AMERICANS

Mexican Americans have some of the same problems the blacks have - poverty and discrimination. However, the degree is not the same. It is a lot easier for a Mexican American to succeed than it is for a black. Poverty plays a large part in keeping some Mexican Americans from better educating themselves. For those who are held back because of their environment and poverty, we should do the same for them that we have suggested we do for the blacks. Bus some of them to predominately white schools, but not the same schools we bussed the blacks to. The two races don't always get along too well with each other. Then for the very bright who are held back by poverty, we should have boarding schools for them, and for the Anglos who are handicapped by poverty.

Poverty and environment are not the only problems the Mexican Americans have. For example, many Mexican Americans and their ancestors who have lived in the United States all their lives, still speak Spanish in their homes and to each other. As a result their children do not have a good English vocabulary, and they speak English with an accent when they enter school, or speak no English at all. This is a handicap children should not have to live with. European and Asian immigrants knew that their success in America depended upon their children speaking English without an accent. So, they demanded that their next generation speak fluent English. All of us speaking the same language has been a very large factor in making this country great. Now there are some Mexican American organizations who are fighting for their right to speak Spanish. We would have to agree that this is their right, but with the same breath, we must forcefully tell them that they are handicapping their children by speaking Spanish in their homes. Their children will very likely speak English with an accent. If they do, they will have at least one strike against them when they start looking for a job. They will also have a limited English vocabulary which may result in two strikes.

How do we overcome this problem? We can't solve all of the problems, but we can help. The Anglos are trying to help by making English the official language of the United Sates. Some Mexican American organizations are fighting this tooth and nail. Adopting English as our official language will go a long way to get Mexican Americans to speak English. But it will not cure the problem. We need

Mexican American leaders to lend a hand. If we can find Mexican Americans who will tell their race the facts of life, they can do more than anyone else can. So far there have been no volunteers.

English has replaced French as the diplomatic language, and English has replaced German as the scientific language. English has always been the language of commerce. Europeans have adopted English as their second language for communicating and trading with each other. English is also the official language of the airways. Airports which handle international traffic must have a control tower operator on duty who can speak English.. Also, every pilot who flies an aircraft into international airports must be able to speak English. Sea ports which are used by ships from foreign countries must have pilots who can speak English. Ships which travel to international ports must be Captained by a person who can speak English. We are well on our way toward adopting English as a common language throughout the world, However, we can't get our Mexican Americans to adopt English as their language. Ironic isn't it?

ANGLOS

This book would not be complete, if it did not address the needs of many Anglos. As we have seen from the SAT scores, there are many Anglos who need to be better educated. If you don't believe the SAT scores, you should drive through some of our country where poverty and welfare prevails. You will see the results of poverty, and you will recognize the poor education of these people when you speak to them. One way of helping those who have the ability to receive higher education would be to place them in boarding schools like those we have recommended for the African Americans and the Mexican Americans. We shouldn't put all disadvantaged in the same schools. We must mix some bright Anglos and minorities in each of the boarding schools which have been recommended. However, the bright Anglos and minorities should be carefully screened to determine whether they are suitable role models.

Not all of the low Anglo SAT scores come from the poor areas. Some of them come from the middle class and the wealthy areas. For those, we should give no special consideration. They are making their own bed, so let them lie in it.

VOUCHERS

Past President Bush advocated the use of vouchers as a means of curing some of our education problems. He would have required that school districts give any of their students who want to attend some other school, a voucher that could be used in any other school in or out of the district. The face value of the voucher would be the amount of money the district receives and spends on each student. The school which received the voucher would receive the value of the voucher as additional income. This amount would be deducted from the funds of the district which issued the voucher.

The idea is not half- bad. It would wake up some

districts, if they were to begin issuing too many vouchers. Also, it could benefit both minorities and Anglos, if they wanted to attend a school which they thought was better than the school to which they were assigned. Students could use the voucher to attend any school of their choice including private schools. Of course, the parents would probably have to pay more than the value of the voucher, if their children elected to attend a private or parochial school. On second thought the idea is a whole lot better than half- bad. It's a good idea, but is going to be hard to sell. School officials and teacher unions will be against it.

MANDATORY EDUCATION UNTIL 18 YEARS OLD

In the Chapter on Compulsory Education we said we must have a National Law which would require compulsory education for everyone until 18 years old, and that we must have separate academic, technical, and trade channels starting at the sixth grade. We also said we would need a channel for incorrigibles, and a separate channel for slow learners. If we establish these channels, and pass a law requiring school attendance until a student is eighteen years old, or has graduated from high school, we can educate everyone at least to some extent. That's a lot better than we are doing today, or will do in the future, under our present system.

MINORITY POPULATION GROWTH

Many Mexican American and African American families produce more children than they can afford. This keeps these families in poverty which, in turn, keeps them from educating all of their children. Even before mid-century this will create a problem unless we develop a plan to educate our minorities, and develop a plan to reduce the birth rate of our minorities. Oh boy! We opened up a can of worms with that statement. However, someone must make the statement, and someone must take the lead, if we are going to educate and feed all of our minorities. We've made the statement. Who will take the lead?

There are ways to help families keep from having more children than they can support and educate, but the solutions are not acceptable to most families. Therefore, in this book, we will concentrate on educating all of our minorities. We haven't been able to do this to date, but we must find a solution. If we do not, we can expect that the percentage of poor, uneducated, and hungry will increase as the minority population increases, and by mid-century, the problem will be explosive. Our country is so far in debt now that we can't properly feed all of our poor. There is no way we can ever get rid of the huge National debt. Therefore, by mid-century, or even before, we are going to have a problem we cannot solve. Wake up, America!

What happens to a country where a large part of the population is hungry? They demand a change. What kind of change will they demand? They will demand a change in leadership. Who will they select as their leader? We don't know, but we do know they will select anyone who says they can feed them.

During the great depression, we followed the right leader, but we came closer to following the wrong leader than most people realize. Following the wrong leader happened in Germany and in Russia when many citizens in these countries were hungry. The same mistake could be made here, so we had better educate all of our citizens so they can make a living in this world, and can select the right leaders for our country.

Some will say "let the minorities lift themselves by their boot straps - we did it this way - why can't they do the same?" The answer is very simple for many of our minorities - they don't have boots. This is one of the problems we must correct.

ATHLETICS

This subject is included in the chapter on minorities, because many minorities choose athletics as their way out of poverty. It is not the way for many. In fact, it is a way of continuing poverty for the many who do not make it to the pros, and most do not make it to the pro ranks.

Once upon a time in the long ago, athletics in schools was used to exercise the students, give them an opportunity to compete with each other, and to compete with other schools. This served useful purposes. It helped the students to maintain their health, and when competing with other schools, it gave them a sense of pride and a sense of belonging.

This picture has changed over the years. In high

school the student athletes still compete with each other and with other schools, but many high school athletes, especially minorities, live in the hope that they will be granted an athletic scholarship to a college. To go to college is a noble goal, but most of them don't want to go to college to receive an education, they want to become star athletes in college so they will be drafted to play in the pros. The colleges don't give athletic scholarships to help someone get a college education, they give the scholarships as pay for semi- professional athletes. The colleges use football and basketball athletes to promote the school, and to make money for the colleges. This is wrong. We should send students to college to get an education, not to make money for the school.

Some minorities think that athletics can get them out of the sink hole of poverty. Their thinking is wrong. Only about one out of one thousand school athletes will be drafted by the pros. In junior high schools and in high schools, this fact must be made known to the students who aspire to become professional athletes, especially to football and basketball players.

Based on statistics, most young athletes will not become professionals. It is cruel to let them go through public school thinking that they don't have to study, because they think they are going to make it in the professional leagues. This fact must be drilled into them while they are young enough to change their goal in life. To do otherwise would be an injustice to the students.

Some small effort is being made to down-play athletics in public schools. For example, some schools have adopted a "no pass- no play" rule. This has helped some, but more needs to be done. A student who barely passes is not going to be able play football in college, and get a meaningful degree. Many students who aspire to become professional athletes take easy courses in high school so they can't be short-stopped by the "no pass-no play" rule. They may get a college athletic scholarship by doing this, but it won't get them an education.

The National Collegiate Athletic Association (NCAA) has recognized this fact, and has adopted minimum standards for granting an athletic scholarship. A student's grade point average must be at least 2.0, and the SAT score must be at least 700. A person with that grade point average and SAT score is about as smart as a barn yard rooster. Such a student probably can't read at the eighth grade level and understand what he has read. That is about the educational level of some college athletes. Of course, there are exceptions - some college athletes have become Rhodes Scholars, and some graduate with a high grade point average, but none of these scholars entered college with a 2.0 grade average and a 700 score on the SAT. They were smart before they entered college, and were able to study and play in college athletics.

The NCAA has also made other changes, but again, not enough to change the semipro status of college athletes. For example, they have eliminated athletic dormitories. The purpose of this change was to insure that athletes mixed with other students. The benefit of this change is at least questionable. Another change was the reduction of practice time for athletes so they would have more time to study. We don't know whether coaches comply with this rule, but even if they do, after a hard practice on a football field or a basketball court, are we to think the athletes are ready to study? Of course they are not, and, what good would it do, if they were ready for study? Not much. Remember most of them would not have been accepted for college entrance, if they had not been very good athletes. In place of being sent to college to play as semipro athletes, these students should have been sent to a job training school where they could be taught a trade which would provide a living for them for the rest of their lives.

Only about 56% of all college athletes graduate after six, repeat, six years in college. Only about 45% of football and basketball players graduate with a degree after six years. Of those who do graduate, most of them do not graduate with a degree that will make them a living, if they are not drafted by the pros. Also, if they are drafted by the pros, they are not assured that they will be able to make a career out of athletics. Many will not be able to perform at the professional level, and some will suffer a disabling injury before reaching retirement age.

We can no longer support semiprofessional athletes in public colleges. We need those college spaces to train engineers, scientists, mathematicians, and other personnel which our country needs. How do we make the necessary changes? We face the facts that colleges hire semipros to bring glory and money to their school. Colleges should hire the best athletes, not students, they can, and use them to make money and bring glory to the school.

The governors of each state should take it on themselves to change the athletic scholarship requirements of each public college in their state. The education requirements should be raised to a level which give college athletes an opportunity to compete in athletics, and an opportunity to graduate with a meaningful degree. Of course, governors of all the states must do this or the change won't be effective. Good luck, Governors.

A FORECAST

Before leaving the chapter on minorities, we must raise a red flag concerning the rapid growth of our two largest minority groups, and of the problems involved in educating them. If we were to compare our country to a human body that was sick, we would find that poor education is a disease which must be treated in order to keep it from becoming an inoperable malignancy. We must take action now to prevent this from happening. If we don't move now, our country will not be the same as we know it by mid-century. It will be a country that cannot compete in the world, and a large percentage of it's population will be uneducated and hungry. Do you remember what happened to Germany and Russia when many of their citizens were hungry? Again, the same could happen to this country. In the year

2050, the person standing next to you, no matter where you are standing, will probably be a minority who is uneducated, unemployed, and hungry, if we cannot solve the problem of educating our minorities.

Wake up, America! You are on a sinking ship, but don't panic. Do as mariners do - stay with the ship until it sinks out from under you. But before it sinks out from under us, let's all get busy on the most important tasks that the United States is faced with - educating our minorities and reducing their birth rate.

Before closing the chapter on minorities, the authors would be remiss, if they did not address the loyalty and patriotism of our minorities.

During WWII we incarcerated our citizens who were of Japanese ancestry. We should be forever shameful for this act. Many of Japanese ancestry who did serve in the armed forces during WWII, served with distinction.

Native Americans served with distinction. The Navahos used their language in messages being sent by our forces so the enemy could not read them. The ploy worked to perfection.

Many Mexican Americans also served with distinction, and quite a number of them were awarded many medals, including the Congressional Medal of Honor. We owe a great debt to these minorities.

Prior to and during WWII we would not let most

African Americans serve in combat, because we thought they would not be good combat soldiers. We did form the 99th Pursuit Group which was manned by African American pilots. They performed admirably in combat.

Immediately after the Civil War, the 24th and 25th infantry, and the 9th and 10th cavalry were formed. All of the enlisted personnel were African Americans. These military units severed to help Anglos settle the West, and to give Anglos a freedom which these brave soldiers were denied. Eighteen of these brave "Buffalo" soldiers were awarded the Congressional Medal of Honor. During WWII only a few of these distinguished soldiers were allowed to enter combat. Most of them served in support units. Shame on us!

OUR MINORITIES ARE AN IMPORTANT PART OF OUR POPULATION, AND WE MUST DO EVERYTHING WE CAN TO HELP MAKE THEM TO BE A VITAL PART OF OUR WORK FORCE. IN ORDER TO DO THIS, WE MUST EDUCATE EVERYONE OF THEM.   IF YOU ARE A MINORITY AND WANT THE BETTER THINGS IN LIFE, AND DO NOT WANT TO LIVE WITH DISCRIMINATION, YOU MUST DO THREE THINGS;

1. SPEAK STANDARD ENGLISH
2. EDUCATE YOURSELF
3. CONDUCT YOURSELF LIKE A MAINSTREAM AMERICAN

CHAPTER XII

LANGUAGE

In the chapter on minorities, we stressed the need for all of us to speak the same language - English. All high school graduates must have a good English vocabulary before entering the workplace or college. Now we must concentrate on getting all students to speak English without an accent, and for them to have an extensive English vocabulary so they can communicate effectively. This ability is a must, if a person is to succeed in the business world, or enter into advanced studies in college.

As America began to expand in business and agriculture, a need for more people became necessary. In order to have enough workers to fill the jobs which were created, we began to import labor. Most of the immigrants who came to our shores did not speak English, but they soon found that they must learn English, if they were going to succeed in their new country. The first generation mastered some of the English language, but spoke with an accent. The next generation attended public schools where they were immersed in the English language from their first day of school. The result was that they were able to graduate and to speak the English language without an accent. This total immersion of immigrants in our language was one of the most important reasons for our becoming the great country which we are today.

Many of our Mexican American citizens speak

Spanish at home even though they have learned some English which they speak with an accent. This makes it almost impossible to turn out a Mexican American student who has the necessary English vocabulary, and who does not speak with an accent. If anyone doubts this statement, they should visit a school where most of the students are Mexican Americans. Here they will find few, if any, who can speak English without an accent. Also, while in the area, one should speak with the local citizens. One will find that most of the Hispanics cannot speak English without an accent. Also, they will find that the Spanish is used by most locals when conversing with each other. The problem is compounded by bilingual education being used in schools much more than is necessary or beneficial. Eliminating, or limiting bilingual education is going to be a very difficult task for three reasons: one, school districts receive federal government money to pay bilingual teachers, and the districts look on this money as being "free money"; two, the teachers who teach bilingual classes want to keep on teaching bilingual classes; three, the Mexican American community wants schools to keep on teaching bilingual classes.

Bilingual education is not the way to have all of us speaking the same language, and speaking it without an accent. Anyone who has tried to learn another language has found that they are not successful until they go to the country where the language is spoken, and become totally immersed in the language. For example, when the State Department wants to train one of their employees to speak a new language, they send the employee to a school where neither the student nor the teacher is permitted to speak English. By using total immersion during language training, the employees arrive in the country where they will be working with a working knowledge of the language. From this point they are able to refine their pronunciation and expand their vocabulary. We should do the same thing with our students - totally immerse them in English from day one in the classroom. This system has worked since the beginning of public schools in the United States. It will work again, if we cut off funds for bilingual education. In fact, cutting funds is the only way we will be able to get rid of bilingual education. Bilingual education is an enemy to education, and one which we must defeat.

In the chapter on minorities, we suggested that we take the very bright students out of their Mexican American or African American environment and place them in boarding schools. If we do this, the language problem could be solved for the students who would be fortunate enough to attend these schools. In these schools we would have very bright Anglos who speak very good English. Mexican Americans and African Americans would soon learn to speak like the Anglos speak - without an accent, and with good pronunciation. Boarding schools will solve many problems concerning minorities, and should be established.

Another way of getting minority students to speak better English is the voucher method of letting students choose their own school. If bright students are permitted to select their own school, they will select the one which they believe will help them the most. We need to do our best to sell the voucher plan. The voucher plan will also help to integrate our schools. Today, we are more segregated in some school districts than we were before we started integration. Students learn from each other, and we should take advantage of this fact.

In order to totally immerse our children in the English language, we must start them to school at the age of three. At that time, very limited bilingual teaching may be used, if necessary. But the goal must be accent free English by the time the student reaches first grade. Then, they will be able to proceed with the English speaking students without being hampered by a language problem. If we don't do this, we will continue to graduate students who don't have the ability to properly communicate. If they can't communicate in English as well as the next person, they will not rise to the level to which they may be capable of rising. They will go through life with this handicap, a handicap which they cannot overcome. Life will be like having one hand tied behind them in a fist fight. Like it or not, that is a fact.

While we are teaching English in kindergarten, we must furnish the parents with material which will help them improve their English, and we must ask them to stop speaking Spanish at home. Many teachers who have taught for a long time along the borders where Spanish is spoken, have been faced with this dilemma - they have started with a new class of students who cannot speak English, and they have found that these children are children of former students who entered school without being able to speak English. Of course, the problem is that speaking Spanish at home is the norm for many Mexican Americans.

Why do we want our students to learn to speak English rather than some other language? The answer is very simple - English is the language that our country uses to conduct business, and what we are trying to teach our students is to be able to hold their own in the real world - the English speaking world.

After NAFTA was passed, many Mexicans who are businessmen in Mexico started taking lessons in English so they could do business with fellow business men from Canada and the United States. If our Mexican American students aspire to become involved in trade with Mexico, they should take Spanish courses in high school and college. Their Tex-Mex, or border Spanish, will not be enough for them to communicate with Mexicans who speak a language which is very close to the original Spanish.

In Europe, each country has its own language. However, most people in the various countries speak English so they can communicate with their very close neighbors. English is the second language in all European countries. In these countries, student instruction in English continues for about six years.

If the rest of the world is adopting English as the

universal language, why shouldn't the United States adopt English as our official language? Of course we should, since it is the language we use to conduct government and commercial business now, and will be the language used in the future.

We are now in the process of taking steps to have the English language be adopted as the official language of the United States. An organization whose name is U.S. English, Inc., is spearheading this effort. The organization was formed a number of years ago by former Senator Hawikawi. To date this organization has been able to have English adopted in many of our states and are working on getting English adopted as our official language in all states and by the Congress of the United States. In the states where English has been adopted, the vote to do so has been by a very large majority.

So, most of the people want English to be adopted as the official language of the United States, but a small minority of special interest groups do not. These groups have fought to prevent the passage of the law. And have brought suits to have the law overturned in the States which have adopted English as their official language. To date they have been unsuccessful, but they keep trying. The organization which is leading the fight to have English as the official language is U.S. English, Inc., 818 Connecticut Ave., Washington, DC 20006.

In this chapter, we haven't touched on Asians, because they are willing to learn English. Therefore, we do not need to consider them when we are trying to get all citizens to read, write, and speak English. The Asians know they must speak the language, if they are going to succeed in this country.

There is one other language problem which we must address in this chapter, and that is the speech used by many African Americans. Their manner of speaking must be changed so that their speech will be accepted by schools and industry. If they don't, they will have one hand tied behind their backs just as the Mexican Americans will have, if they don't learn to speak English without an accent. Do you know a Mexican American or an African American who has become successful in business or government who does not speak standard English?

A language problem similar to the one Canada has could be ours also, if we don't head it off by requiring all citizens to speak English. By the middle of the next century about one half of our population will be what we now call minorities. The largest percentage of the minorities will be Mexican Americans and African Americans. We can't get them to speak correct English today in their homes, and to each other. This fact results in their poor living conditions, and creates a problem with trying to educate their children. Just think of how much the problem will be magnified by mid-century, if we don't find a way to convince our two largest minority groups that they are hurting themselves, and their children by not learning to speak standard English. How do we solve this problem? No one knows, but we had better find a solution now not next year. The very foundation of our country rests on all of us being educated, and on all of us being able to speak the same language fluently.

Also, we have not found a solution for educating all of our two major minorities. Today about 25% of the Mexican American and African American students drop out of school. Think about what problems our country will have when about one half of the population will be minorities, and many of them will be uneducated and poor. All of the jobs which do not require an education or a skill will nearly all be gone, and the few remaining jobs will probably be exported where they can be done for less money. How will we feed, shelter, and clothe our minorities? We can hardly support the welfare program now, and the problem could grow to an enormous problem before mid-century. This is a problem which everyone must recognize, and start doing something about now.

The thing we must do about the problem beginning right now is to tell the minorities the facts of life. Who will volunteer to do this?

WE CAN'T MAKE THIS COUNTRY GREAT AGAIN, IF WE DON'T ALL SPEAK THE SAME LANGUAGE. ALSO, WE CAN'T LEARN TO GET ALONG WITH EACH OTHER, IF WE CAN'T COMMUNICATE, AND WE CANT COMMUNICATE, IF WE DON'T SPEAK THE SAME LANGUAGE.

CHAPTER XIII

CURRICULA

As the authors stated in Chapter IV "GOALS 2000: Educate America Act", standards, curricula, and tests should have been prepared by the federal government for the states to use as guides. Without such guidance, public schools will probably continue to go down hill as they have done since our public education system began to fail us in 1963. Our educators have had over thirty years to get education back on track. It is hoped that we have reached the low point in education - high school graduates who can't read at the eighth grade level, who don't understand what they have been taught, who don't know where any of the worlds' countries are located, who can't do simple two part arithmetic problems, fractions and decimals, and who rank near the bottom when compared with students from fourteen other countries.

The GOALS 2000 Act establishes goals to be attained by students, but doesn't tell the schools how to accomplish the goals. The authors think the 400 or more million dollars of federal government money given to schools each year to improve education is going to be wasted since our schools were not told how to accomplish the goals. So, lets get on with this chapter so we can address what we can do without guidelines.

UPGRADED CURRICULA

GOALS 2000 has begun measuring accomplishment toward achieving the goals established by the Act. Curricula in our schools must be upgraded in order for our schools to begin to achieve the goals which have been established. Curriculum for subjects such as English, history, geography, mathematics, and science are subjects which will require a great deal of upgrading. Not only must the curriculum for each subject be upgraded, the teaching must also be upgraded. Many of our teachers who teach these subjects are not qualified to teach the subjects, and do not know how to teach the relevance of the subjects to the real world. Students are to be measured by GOALS 2000 in these subjects. Public school administrators, you must get on the ball and start moving and shaking.

The curricula in all public schools must be upgraded. As was shown in Chapter II "How Bad?", our top students are very far behind top students in many countries of the world in math and science. This means that our teaching level is too low. Statistics reported by the Scholastic Achievement Test organization indicate that grades given to students are normal. Therefore, we can assume that we are letting the students set the standards. We not only need to bring our teaching up to world standard, we must continually update as more and more knowledge becomes available.

A major change we must make in our education system is to provide academic and technical training for high school graduates who will have to go to work after graduation. We have failed miserably in this area. We must provide technical/trade courses

136

which will teach students who are not going to college, a trade or a skill which will help them get a job when they graduate from high school. GOALS 2000 has established under Title V a board composed of educators, business leaders, and industry personnel who will provide guidance for the establishment of, and the curricula for, the technical/trade channels. We need technicians as well as engineers and scientists. School districts need to start now to establish these channels. The new channels will require money to properly set them up, but maybe some of the sub-grant money for local reform could be used for this purpose. Also, local industry and business may provide some of the equipment, etc., which will be necessary.

STANDARDIZED CURRICULA

Curricula must be standardized in public schools for every grade from kindergarten through the eighth grade for two reasons. The most important reason is that all high school graduates should graduate with the same academic qualifications, no matter what school they graduated from. Another reason is that many children will change schools during their public school years. Therefore, we must have standardized course materials for all grades in all schools in the United States, so that student transferees will be able to enter a new school and continue the learning process without causing more trauma than the move itself has caused.

Many of our youth will transfer several times during their public school years. Many will find they are ahead or behind in the school they transfer to. Those who find themselves ahead of where they were in the school they came from will become bored, and this could lead to other problems. Those who find themselves behind will suffer the most. They will have a rough time trying to play catch up, or they may have to be placed in a lower grade. Whether they find themselves behind or ahead, these children may have their attitude toward school altered for life. Children do not like to leave their homes and their friends. Transferring children to a new school is a trying time for parents and their children. Let's not make it an even more trying time by teaching different subjects at the same grade level in different schools.

Students from military families are an example of where children change schools very often. Many other families also move three or four times during their children's public school years.

The effect on students is a compelling reason for standardizing the academic curricula , but an even better reason is the fact that GOALS 2000 will be reporting on progress being made toward achieving the goals established by the ACT. If students in each state are to be measured against students in other states, we must start standardizing curricula in all states.

STANDARDIZING CURRICULA

We cannot let the states prepare their versions of standardized curricula for two reasons; one, we would probably end up with a Babel situation again;

two, we don't have time to start from scratch, because time is of the essence since we are so far behind in educating our children. Since the federal government is not going to furnish sample curricula, etc., each state should look for curricula which has proven itself. Many private schools have courses which turn out students who are much better qualified than most public school students. Why not borrow their curricula? Also, there are correspondence schools who have good courses of instruction. One such school is the Calvert School which is located in Baltimore, Maryland. Parents who have used the Calvert School material have been well-pleased. One of the authors used the material for instructing her children at home and found that they skipped a grade when they went back to public school.

If proper arrangements are made with the Calvert School, the course material could be used to quickly upgrade the curricula in public schools. The Calvert School home study curricula is pointed out only to illustrate that a good curricula is available to use as a guide. There are other home study courses which may be as good, or better, and any district which would like to improve on their curricula should contact all home study providers, Also, there are home study providers whose curricula is Bible based. Parents who do not want their children to be exposed to the secular teaching of public schools should contact providers of Bible based study courses. The School of Tomorrow which is located in Lewisville, Texas, has Bible based courses. These courses are used in a large number of places in the old Soviet Union - the "Evil Empire." It is ironic that the Evil Empire is using Bible based course material and we can't even mention the Bible in our schools. That must change and will be changed in time. Let's hope it is changed before we become a Sodom and Gomorrah.

The course materials from all home study providers come with teaching guides which can be used by teachers to prepare standardized lesson plans. If this is done, teachers will not be burdened by preparing new lesson plans every time they are moved from one grade to another. This will also make it easier for teachers to move along with their students as their students move to a higher grade. More on this in the Chapter on "Teachers and Administrators."

We hope that the state education agencies will work with college instructors who teach freshman classes to help them in determining what every freshman should know before entering college. We now have too many college freshmen taking remedial courses. After the state education agencies have developed standards for college bound students, each school district should develop course materials which would prepare students for college entrance.

Students have been setting the teaching standard as evidenced by the SAT scores and the "Bell Curve" grades given to students. Another fact which proves that public school teaching level is too low is the fact that a great number of college freshmen must take remedial course in math, science, reading, writing, and geography.

The knowledge which becomes available to us doubles about every twelve years. No one in our education system has done anything about incorporating increased knowledge into our public school courses. Curricula personnel should make note of all new discoveries and advancements which have occurred in the past year, and should make changes in the curricula to incorporate the teaching of this new knowledge. Encyclopedia publishers issue an update every year. These updates contain information which educators should use to update what is being taught in their schools.

TECHNICAL/TRADE CURRICULA

In the Chapter on Minorities and Athletes, we stressed the need for technical/trade channels to begin at the sixth grade. Therefore, we don't need to justify the creation of these channels in this chapter. However, we do need to cover how the course material for these channels will be developed. We must get industry and business personnel involved in the development of these courses. The GOALS 2000 Act establishes a board to do just this. We don't have educators who are familiar with requirements of industry and business for their entry level personnel. Therefore, we must rely on industry personnel from all industries for which we plan to establish a training program. For example, if we want to establish an electronic technician course, we must have personnel from companies who use electronic technicians to help us write the course material.

141

The use of industry personnel will be easy to obtain, because industry spends millions of dollars each year on training programs which teach what their entry level personnel should have learned in public schools. Business and industry want their new personnel to be trainable, and to have the necessary background for training before they are hired, not after they are hired. This job is the job of public schools, and a job which is not being done today. The only way we can fill this requirement is to establish technical/trade channels which have been developed by industry personnel who will hire our students when they graduate.

Not all school districts will be able to have courses for all technical/trade channels which will be required to fill the demand for technicians in all fields, but it may be feasible for every school district to establish at least one such program. Therefore, students must be permitted to transfer to any school, in or out of their district, where the courses they want to pursue are available. This brings us back to the need for vouchers for our students. All students should be able to transfer to any other school, if the student thinks a better education program is offered in the school of their choice.

We have not addressed curricula which will be needed to train the slow learners and the incorrigibles. Before we start on the curricula for these student groups, we should get the best minds which are available to assist in preparation of the course materials. These two groups must be educated to the fullest extent possible, because they are also needed in the work force.

TECHNICAL/TRADE CHANNELS WILL PRO-
VIDE THE BEST SOLUTION FOR EDUCATING
THE MAJORITY OF STUDENTS WHO CANNOT, OR
ARE NOT QUALIFIED TO, GO TO COLLEGE.
THESE CHANNELS ALSO WILL PROVIDE WORK-
ERS FOR JOBS WHICH ARE IN DEMAND, AND DO
NOT REQUIRE A COLLEGE EDUCATION. O N E
WAY OR ANOTHER, WE MUST STANDARDIZE
INSTRUCTION IN ALL PUBLIC SCHOOLS.

CHAPTER XIV

TEACHERS AND ADMINISTRATORS

Teachers are our first line of defense against ignorance. Therefore, they are our second most valuable asset - our children being our most valuable. Before the decline of the family, mothers were our second most valuable asset, because they were the ones who taught, loved, raised, and disciplined our children. Today, too many mothers do not really qualify as mothers. Some of them qualify more as incubators, because they have a child and immediately go to work and leave the child raising to someone else. Teachers are the bottom line in our education system. Sometimes we want to blame our teachers for the sad condition of our schools. If we do, we are aiming at the wrong target. If we have to place blame, it must be directed at the family, the Supreme Court who ruled out prayer in our schools, and the school administrators who have not only not been able to solve the school problems, but who, in many cases, have contributed to the problems.

In order to improve education in our schools, we must work from the bottom up. We must start with the teachers, and the first start we must make is to pay the good teachers more, and fire the ones who are not up to teacher standards. For too long we have not paid our good teachers a living wage. They have been forced to work at after school jobs or during the vacation period when they should have been able to recuperate from the long teaching period during the nine month school year. If we pay our teachers a living wage, we can attract better qualified personnel to be teachers, and we can attract more men to be teachers. Why do we need more men to become teachers? We need them so that students will be exposed to men and women during their education years. Students from one parent families especially need to be exposed to men , because most of these students come from a family headed by a woman. When these students reach marriage age they have not been taught and disciplined by a man. Therefore, they do not know how to cope with the sex they have not been exposed to.

If we are going to pay our teachers more, we should expect more from them. And, we can get more from them, if we give them more authority. We need to let them become part of the solution by letting them have a voice in setting school district policies. Teachers know what dress code the students should comply with, they know what the disciplinary policy should be, they know what the curriculum should be for the grade they are teaching. They know all of the things the district should do to improve education in the district. Any district which does not use this wealth of information is not using the tools they have available to them, and are treating their teachers as if they were merely the ones who dispense the district policies and are not qualified to be a part of the policy process. District superintendents, you should have a meeting of all teachers the next time you want to set a standard, or establish a policy. You'll find a great deal of talent which will help you make a good decision and make your district better.

Teachers know the deficiencies which their students come to their grade with. They know whether students are deficient in some subjects which have been taught before they received the students. Teachers should be required to prepare a memo concerning the deficiencies which they have observed in newly assigned students. Administrators should use the memos to correct teaching deficiencies. If all school districts used this method of improving education in their districts, they would see an improvement in test scores and teaching. Let's get the teachers involved in improving education.

Now that we have begun to use our teachers to the utmost of their ability, we need to address the method used to select our principals, counselors, curricula personnel, and school superintendents. Most states will not promote a classroom teacher to be a principal unless the teacher has the required administrative courses. Another example is that a classroom teacher cannot be promoted to be a counselor unless the teacher has had the required counselor courses. Likewise a teacher cannot be promoted to a job in curricula development, if the teacher has not had all of the curricula development courses which are required. To all of this nonsense, the authors say - HOGWASH. Any good teacher who knows how to motivate and discipline will make a better principal than one whose only asset is required courses. Some schools hire counselors who have not had any classroom teaching experience.

How can such a person do a good job of counseling? They can't, and any good classroom teacher can do a better job than many of our so called counselors. Who knows the changes which must be made in the curriculum better than a classroom teacher. The experience of classroom teachers should be used in the development of curriculum in the field of their expertise.

We should promote good classroom teachers to be principals rather than teachers who have had administrative courses. This foolish way of selecting principals is one of the reasons for lack of control in our schools. Many of those selected to be principals do not have the ability to motivate students and to discipline them. We need principals who can control students, inspire teachers, get parents involved, and maintain discipline. If we don't have teachers who can be promoted to this very vital cog in the education machinery, we should hire Marine Corps retired Colonels. They have taught, inspired, and disciplined all of their career. District superintendents should note this and replace unsatisfactory principals with retired Marine Colonels. They will get discipline back on track so that classroom teachers can teach.

In summary, we should pay our good teachers a living wage, and should use their ability to improve our education system. Also, we should promote our classroom teachers based on their ability - not on the courses they have taken. This will be flying into the face of "educators" in the state education agencies, but it must be done, no matter what it takes to do it. We will not see very much improvement in education, if we don't utilize the most qualified to supervise education.

In the chapter on colleges, we will address the changes colleges must make.

CHAPTER XV

TEACHER COLLEGES

Yes, we know that "teacher colleges" have been "outlawed", but they are still out there buried inside a college or university. They are not only still out there, but they are teaching the same old theories which were taught in the teacher colleges before they were "outlawed." What are these theories? They are modern day versions of theories expounded in the past by such characters as Wilhelm Max Wundt, James Cattell, the National Education Association's Commission on Reorganization of Secondary Education, A.K.A. The Gang of Seven, the disciples who have followed these "educators" and other education "nuts".

Our state supported colleges have the freedom to teach any courses that appeal to them, and for which they have funds, instructors, equipment, and classroom space. As a result, many state supported colleges offer degrees in fields that are not in demand in today's exploding technological and service world. For example, our colleges turn out ten lawyers for every engineer. In Japan, just the reverse is true - ten engineers are graduated for every lawyer who is graduated. As everyone knows, we are overloaded with lawyers, and are short on mathematicians, scientists, computer engineers, engineers, trade economists, and engineering technicians. This is just one example of where colleges teach courses that do not lead to a career which is in demand in our changing world. Many of those who major in fields such as philosophy, psychology, art, music, etc., are hard pressed to find a job when they graduate, and they have expended many tax payer dollars while being educated in fields which are not in great demand. Many of them have to settle for jobs as clerks in stores, traveling salespersons, car salespersons, real estate salespersons, or some other job which does not require a college degree. Many of the Arts degree graduates will have to work for wages which are near the poverty level.

In the time before the industrial revolution, colleges were for the nobility, the wealthy, and for men of the cloth. Those days are long gone. The goal of today's colleges should be to train everyone who has the capability of earning a meaningful degree. In the early days of the United States, Land Grant Colleges were formed to meet a demand for agricultural and engineering graduates. These colleges did this very well. We are now the foremost food producer in the world thanks to Land Grant, and other agricultural college graduates. The Land Grant Colleges also turned out engineers who were the greatest in the world - but not any more. Somewhere along the line these colleges strayed from the courses they were established to teach, and began turning out music, psychology, philosophy, and art majors, etc. The Land Grant Colleges need to have their curricula changed to where they are teaching the courses for which they were established. This change must also be made in other state supported colleges that graduate students in fields for which there is no demand. Colleges today should be staffed and equipped to train in the professions which are required to make this country great again. And, we say again, because we have lost our standing in education and technology in the world to countries we once thought to be "backward." Before WWII we even included Japan in this category.

We cannot continue to use taxpayers money to teach students who do not have the talent to pursue courses for which there is a demand. We can no longer use our college facilities for students who want to go to college just so they can say they graduated from college. If these students want to go to college to study courses for which there is not a demand in industry, they should go to private colleges which are staffed to teach courses in the arts, and are not staffed and equipped to teach technical courses.

Studies are made every year to determine what fields are in demand, but colleges probably do not even have a copy of these studies, or if they do, they keep on teaching the same old courses. This cannot continue. Changes must be made, but the changes will not come easily. The demand for change must come from taxpayers, and must be supported by the Governors of each state. The Governors must be involved, because they are the ones who can put pressure on the legislative branches to make the changes. And, the legislative bodies will not take action to make the changes, if the taxpayers and the Governors do not support and demand the changes. We must have the legislatures behind the change, because they control the funds, and the ones who control the funds are the only ones who can order the changes.

We can't ask the colleges to make the changes for many reasons, one being they have a vested interest in continuing as they are. To drop or lower enrollment in any of the courses they are now teaching would probably require that they dismiss some instructors and professors who may have tenure. To do that would be a chore that college presidents do not have the authority to do except in rare cases, and they do not want to upset the apple cart, even if they do have the authority. These obstacles must be removed so the presidents can make the necessary changes. Each Governor and legislative branch must decide on how to take care of surplus instructors and professors. One way would be to retire those who are eligible, and to lower the retirement requirements for those who are near retirement age and length of service. Also, some could be used in other branches of the state government. Still others could be used in the state education agencies to assist in strengthening high school courses so that graduates will be ready to enter college, and to pursue a course at college level rather than at the remedial level, or will be ready to enter the workplace ready to work.

Again, let us state, some colleges have as many as 50% of their freshmen taking remedial courses. Of course, these students should never have been accepted by the college, but they were for various reasons. Colleges should begin to raise their admission standards now. This will, in turn, help to raise the graduation standards in high schools. And, we will see better qualified high school graduates in the future, if we follow the courses for changes which are being discussed in this book.

A realigning of courses offered at public colleges is not the only change which must be made. There are many, but in this chapter we will deal only with those which affect education. We will begin with changes which must be made in teacher training. First, teachers must be able to teach two subjects when they graduate. One of the subjects should be mathematics or science. We have too many English and history teachers. The minimum science course should be a general course covering physics, chemistry, biology, and anatomy. The math course should be algebra, trigonometry, and geometry at above the high school level. Also, every student who wants to become a teacher should have a course in computers and geography before graduation.

After the students have mastered basic courses which they will teach in schools when they graduate, they must be given a course in teacher training. The course should be about 180 classroom hours in length and should cover how to control classes, how to teach a subject, and how to motivate. They should not be courses in education. If persons know a subject, they can be taught what they need to know about teaching in a very short time. In fact, if a mathematician were hired to teach a mathematics course, he or she would need little, if any, teacher training. Teachers do not need to know "theories" of education which are, at best, "invented soft science theories". These "theories" have been invented so that a person could be awarded a masters or doctors degree in education. These degrees must be abolished. If teachers aspire to better educate themselves, the subject they teach should be the one in which they should take advanced courses. Or, they should take courses in a related field - not courses in education.

At the present time many school districts are having trouble hiring teachers who are able to teach science and math courses. The reason being that most who go to school to become teachers do not graduate with expertise in these subjects. We can satisfy this demand by hiring military personnel who are being released due to down sizing of the military. There are many skills which these people have, and they have had the teaching and disciplinary training which will enable them to control students, if the administrators will let them. If we pursue the course of hiring people who are qualified in their field, we do not need to demand that they take "X" number of college hours in education courses. In fact, many will enter the classroom, and perform better than the education majors who are now teaching. Remember, these people have been teaching others during their entire military career. And, if they need some training in procedures, etc., they can be given that instruction by teacher trainers in the school districts.

In addition to eliminating most of the education theories now being taught, we must concentrate on teaching subject matter, so that teachers will be experts in their field when they graduate. Also, we must teach prospective teachers to be mother, father, confident, and disciplinarian. The reason for this requirement is simple - teachers need to assume the roll of parents, because as many as 50% of our children do not have full-time parents at home who will give them love, will teach them values, and will discipline them. Therefore, teachers must become vicars for some of the parents.

Children from a family where the mother is head of the household, and the bread winner especially need to be taught by a teacher who can give them love, can teach them right from wrong, can discipline them, motivate them, and teach subjects which all children need to learn. Children want to grow up to be responsible citizens, and they will accept value training and discipline during the growing up process. They don't want to end up in prison or on relief, if the teacher shows them a better way of life. Therefore, teachers must be taught how to motivate, love, and discipline their students. If the teachers do not do this, probably no one else will. This is especially true, if the child comes from a one parent family. The only way schools can take on the responsibility of giving whole training rather than just academic training is to have teachers who have been trained to be parent and teacher. This is a sad, but true.

We can't assume that all teachers will be qualified to assume the new roll they must play as a teacher, because some of them have come from homes where values were not taught, and discipline was not always administered. That is why we must teach future teachers how to be a friend and confidant to their students

Another thing that colleges which have a teacher training program should do is to set a higher academic standard for teacher trainees. At present many teachers graduate in the lower 25% of their class in high school and in college. This gives credence to the old adage that those who can, do, and those who can't, teach. This must be changed. We need to have our brightest in the teaching profession. The lower standard for teachers is causing some of the problems we are having in schools today. When teachers graduate from college, they should have had sufficient training in the subject matter they want to teach so they can hold their own with anyone in the field of their expertise. If they are not experts in their field, they should not be teachers. We want our teachers to be looked up to by their students, by the student's parents, and by society.

When students graduate from college, and want to enter the teaching field, they should be an experts in at least one subject, and should be able to teach at least one other subject. If the major subject is not science or math, the minor subject should be mathematics and science. Too many teachers are limited by their being able to teach only one subject. This limits teacher assignments, and causes tunnel vision. Before students are allowed to begin a major in the teaching field, they should have had high school courses in science and mathematics. They will need these subjects in order to take college courses which will qualify them to teach math or science when they graduate.

Accomplishing the goal of turning out teachers who can teach subjects besides English and history will not be easy. Instructors in colleges who teach education courses will not want to change, but they must. Their students must graduate with enough education training to be able to teach two subjects effectively. It doesn't take a lot of education theory to do this. Colleges will resist incorporating courses which teach how to be a mother, father, confident, counselor, friend, and disciplinarian. They will want to continue teaching the same old subjects which have been taught in teacher colleges for generations. Such training will not get the job done. Also, many of the teacher trainees will not want to concentrate on learning subjects such as math and science, because these are "tough" subjects. Most aspiring teachers are comfortable with learning history and English as their subjects of expertise, and will resist learning other subjects.

One thing that colleges should do is try to encourage more men to become teachers. Our students are taught most of their academic life by female instructors. They need to be exposed to male teachers during their public school years. This is especially true for students who come from a family which is headed by a woman. Of course, colleges will need help in attracting men into the teaching profession. First, they will have to raise the professional level of teachers, and to do this schools will have to pay more to both female and male teachers. Teachers have for too long been paid a wage that they cannot live on. We must change this.

CONCLUSIONS

1. Colleges should drop many education courses.
2. Colleges must teach values to not only teacher trainees, but to all students.
3. Colleges must teach prospective teachers how to be mother, father, confident, friend and counselor to their students.
4. Colleges must raise their entrance standards.
5. Colleges must teach math, geography, and science courses to teacher trainees.
6. Colleges must stop giving degrees in education.
7. Colleges must teach courses which industry wants to be taught.

A REQUIEM FOR PUBLIC COLLEGES

In the preceding paragraphs we touched on the decline of our state colleges. We pointed out that as many as 50% of college freshmen require remedial courses. Also, we pointed out that some teacher trainees may have to be given watered-down math and science courses. This is true for teacher trainees, because most of the students who want to teach do not graduate from high school with a comprehensive knowledge of math and science. This is also true for many other college students. In summary, many students in state colleges must take remedial courses and watered-down college courses. This will mark the beginning of a race to the bottom.

A concrete example of a race to the bottom is the decline of the City College of New York. This College was founded to give the poor, who were qualified, an opportunity to become educated. This purpose was more than fulfilled. The college turned out 11 Nobel Prize winners, and more CEO's than any other university of it's size. General Colin Powell is one of the university's graduates.

The claim to fame ended when the university lowered it's entrance standards so that the student population would be in proportion to the ethnic population of the city. As a result, City College of New York is now close to the bottom of the barrel.

Another example of lowering standards is what the Service Academies have done to accommodate many of the women and minority students. These colleges, the Air Force Academy, the Naval Academy, and West Point have abandoned an all engineering curricula, and have resorted to graduating about one third of the students in the arts such as English, history, social sciences, and psychology, etc. Before integration of women and minorities into the Academies, the curriculum was based on engineering, because the weapons the services use are products of engineering. Therefore , the officers who deployed these weapons needed to know how the weapons were made, and how they functioned. An officer who has majored in social sciences or any other arts degree program will not understand, and be able to deploy the weapons of the services. We are wasting taxpayers money to educate officers who are not properly educated to fight with modern day weapons. We can blame the Women's Lib Movement for handicapping our military with officers who are not properly trained, and with enlisted personnel who can never become the aggressive fighters we need.

In the preceding two paragraphs we have addressed the lowering of standards of City College of New York and the Service Academies. The same applies to almost all of our public colleges and universities - they all have lowered their entrance standards. They have lowered their entrance requirements, because they could not fill their halls of learning with high school graduates who were qualified to enter college. So rather than lowering enrollment, and holding firm on their entrance requirements, they lowered their standards to fit the entering students.

Lowering of standards could continue to where we could send untrained monkeys to college. Well, maybe we would have to give them some training before sending them to college. Or, maybe we won't be able to send them to college - just through high school.

CHAPTER XVI

SUMMARY / CONCLUSIONS

CHAPTER I
"WHY WE MUST EDUCATE EVERYONE"

In this chapter we gave reasons why everyone must be educated. This fact needs to be stressed again, because the world is becoming more and more technical every day. That, of course, means that all jobs except for fast food service, etc., will require an educated or skilled work force. Anyone who is not educated or skilled will not be able to find work, and anyone who can't find work becomes a burden on society. Our country can't support the numbers on welfare that we have today, and we can't put them to work, because most of them are dropouts, and unqualified to do anything except pick and shovel jobs. Unskilled jobs such as screwing on lug nuts in an automobile manufacturing plant have disappeared. As machines replace workers in manufacturing plants, more jobs will disappear, or they will be exported to a country where they can be performed by cheap labor.

By mid-century about half of our population will be minorities. Today about one-forth of the minorities become dropouts. If we can't do better than that, one out of every four people in the United States, by mid-century, will be poor, uneducated, and hungry. We can't afford to support the number of people who are on the relief rolls today. What are we going to do when one-fourth of our citizens are on relief?

Politicians keep talking about reducing the number of people on relief by requiring them to go to work. Where are the jobs that people on relief can do? Politicians should work with the people who are on relief, in order to become acquainted with them. One of the authors did this for four years, and found that very few have a skill which they could use in the job market, even if they were inclined to work.

WE HAD BETTER LEARN HOW TO EDUCATE EVERYONE.

CHAPTER II
"HOW BAD?"

In this chapter we compared our top math and science students to top math and science students from fourteen other countries. In both subjects our students ranked third from the bottom. Countries which ranked first and second in both subjects are Taiwan and Korea. Also, we learned that our students do not know how to apply what little science and math they know, and are unable to work problems which require reasoning. This tells us that our students cannot compete in the technical world. If we cannot compete in the new technical world, our country's future is in jeopardy. The outlook is bleak unless we start making changes in our education system TODAY. We are already behind, and must play catch up as we try to improve our education system. We not only have to play catch up, we must constantly incorporate new technology which doubles about every twelve years.

HOW BAD IS IT? LET'S SAY OUR EDUCATION SYSTEM STINKS.

CHAPTER III
"FAMILY"

In this chapter we learned that the decline of the family is the largest contributor to: the decline in education, the rising crime rate, the increase in divorces, and the increase in immorality. The Supreme Court's ruling out prayer in schools is the second largest contributor to the decline of our nation.

We can't change the composition of our families, but we can make them accountable for their offsprings by requiring that they be responsible for the conduct and education of their children. It has been done in some school districts, and can be done in all districts.

ALMOST EVERYTHING WHICH IS BAD FOR OUR COUNTRY CAN BE TRACED BACK TO THE DECLINE OF THE FAMILY, AND THE SUPREME COURT'S RULING OUT PRAYER IN OUR SCHOOLS.

CHAPTER III
"GOALS 2000: Educate America Act"

This strategy prepared by President Clinton and The Secretary of Education is the first sensible thing the government has done to improve education. The Act was passed by a large bipartisan majority of the Senate and House. The U. S. Department of Education adopted the strategy which has eight goals to be accomplished by the year 2000. Most of these goals cannot be accomplished in such a short time period. However, none of them will be accomplished unless most of the changes offered in this book are made to our school system.

Everyone should have a copy of this Act. If you are interested, write to:

> U. S. Department of Education
> Goals 2000: Educate America Act
> 400 Maryland Ave.
> Washington, DC 20202-0498

The Department of Education will annually prepare reports on how well each state is doing toward meeting the goals of the Act. The reports are in understandable form and will furnish information relative to how our schools and our students are doing. Public school officials should study the reports to determine how their schools are doing, and how improvements could be made.

PUBLIC SCHOOL ADMINISTRATORS, YOU HAD BETTER START SHAPING UP, BECAUSE YOUR STUDENTS ARE GOING TO BE REPORTED ON. IF YOUR STUDENTS DO NOT MEASURE UP TO STANDARD, CONTRACT SCHOOLS, PRIVATE SCHOOLS, OR HOME STUDY MAY REPLACE YOU.

CHAPTER V
"CRIME AND PUNISHMENT"

In this chapter, we saw how crime has increased

dramatically since the Supreme court ruled out prayer in schools in 1962, and how the family has declined since that time. Also, at about that time, our Justices began to water-down our laws. For example, we can no longer give criminals the swift and justified punishment which they deserve. The death penalty is almost impossible to give to even the hardest of criminals, and if given, the criminal stays on death row for years and years while the appeal process goes on. Today we have young barbarians driving cars, and shooting people. We haven't changed our laws so that they can be punished as they should be. Children are killing children. Gang members are killing each other. While all of this killing is going on, we are hog-tied by juvenile laws which were designed to punish juveniles who stole a pack of gum or a bicycle.

We need to wake up, and change our laws so that we can require "an eye for an eye and a tooth for a tooth".

HOW LONG ARE WE GOING TO LET CRIME GO UNCONTROLLED BEFORE WE BRUSH ASIDE THE ACLU AND THE DO-GOODERS, SO WE CAN PUNISH CRIMINALS AS WE SHOULD?

CHAPTER VI
"CHARACTER EDUCATION"

In this chapter we stressed the need for teaching character education in schools. Teaching value training in schools is the only way some of our students are going to be exposed to the subject. Many are not taught right from wrong at home. Incorporating this subject is easy, because a value training program which has been approved by all states, and which does not conflict with the Supreme Court ruling is available.

Most criminals have not had value training in their homes or in their schools before committing their crimes. If we can't teach right from wrong to all youths before they leave school, we can expect the crime rate to continue to rise. We will have barbarians on our streets who will commit murder for pocket change, and some who will become mad bombers such as those who blew up the Federal building in Oklahoma City. Others will join radical militia units.

IF THE SCHOOLS DO NOT GIVE VALUE TRAINING, STUDENTS CANNOT BE CONTROLLED WHILE IN SCHOOL, AND WILL CONTINUE ON THE CRIME PATH MANY JUVENILES HAVE CHOSEN.

CHAPTER VII
"UNIFORMS, PEER PRESSURE, AND SEX"

Wearing uniforms to school will do three things: one, it will instill a sense of pride in the students; two, it will get rid of sexy clothes in classrooms; and three, it will help to eliminate peer pressure which results from some children not being able to dress as well as some of the students. Peer pressure is one cause for some students not doing as well as they could, and for some to drop out of school.

WEARING UNIFORMS TO SCHOOL SHOULD BE GIVEN A HIGH PRIORITY.

CHAPTER VIII
"YEAR-ROUND SCHOOL"

Nine month school was necessary for farmers. Today only 2% of our population lives on farms. In this chapter we listed twelve advantages for having year-round schools. This is almost the twenty-first century. Let's update our schools so we can take advantage of the benefits of year-round school. This change will help us in the war to educate everyone.

TO DATE MANY SCHOOLS HAVE MADE THIS CHANGE. OTHER SCHOOLS SHOULD START TO MAKE THIS CHANGE IMMEDIATELY.

CHAPTER IX
"AFTER SCHOOL ACTIVITIES"

Six good reasons for having after school activities were given in this chapter. One of the best reasons is to keep children off the streets until their parents get home from work. This will help reduce crime, and will give the students an opportunity to participate in games, hobbies, etc., and to take subjects in which they have an interest.

SCHOOLS MUST TAKE ON MORE RESPONSIBILITY THAN JUST ACADEMIC TRAINING. AFTER SCHOOL ACTIVITIES GIVE EDUCATORS THE OPPORTUNITY TO BROADEN THEIR TEACHING TO INCLUDE FUN AND GAMES, AND MORAL TRAINING.

CHAPTER X
"COMPULSORY EDUCATION"

We can't educate everyone, if we can't keep them in the classrooms. A universal law which requires school attendance until a student is eighteen, or has graduated from high school is a must. However, we need to create two channels in addition to the academic channel before we pass the law. One channel would be for technical and trade training, and the other would be for incorrigibles. The technical/trade channel would be for those who cannot relate to Shakespeare, Burns, and "The Ancient Mariner", but can see the advantages of getting technical training. If we had such a law, and other than academic channels, we could educate everyone to some extent.

THIS BALL IS IN THE STATES' COURTS. THEY ARE THE ONES WHO MUST PASS THE LAW AND INCORPORATE THE NEW CHANNELS. GET BUSY, GOVERNORS.

CHAPTER XI
"MINORITIES"

Minorities must receive the most help in our effort to educate everyone, because we are not able to educate about one-forth of them today. This must change, because the minorities will almost be the majority by mid-century. If we can't do better, one forth of our population will be uneducated, hungry, and on relief by the year 2050.

WE MUST START NOW TO DO WHATEVER IS NECESSARY TO EDUCATE ALL OF OUR MINORI-

TIES. WE NEED THEM IN THE WORKPLACE, NOT ON RELIEF ROLLS, BUT THEY MUST FIRST BE EDUCATED, BECAUSE THERE WILL BE NO JOBS FOR THE UNEDUCATED OR UNSKILLED IN THE NEXT CENTURY.

CHAPTER XII
"LANGUAGE"

We must all be able to speak the same language, if our country is going to remain strong. If we can't communicate, we can't cooperate, and the cooperation of everyone is necessary, if we are going to be able to compete in our new and technical world.

Mexican Americans would like to continue speaking Spanish in their homes and to each other. Therefore, their communication skill in English is hampered by their accent, and by their limited English vocabulary. English has almost become the universal language in the world, but we can't get all of our citizens to speak it fluently.

Many African Americans do not try to speak standard English. That is one cause for discrimination. Most Anglos don't want English, as spoken by many African Americans, to be brought into the schools and the workplace.

Every school should have a course in voice communication where students could be taught correct pronunciation and oral delivery.

Let's all get on the band wagon to get English adopted as our official language. This won't solve the language problem, but it will help, and we need all the help we can get.

One subject which wasn't addressed in this Chapter is the deterioration of the English language as spoken by Anchor persons, etc., who should speak perfect English, because their listeners are learning from them. You have heard their mistakes, but a few reminders are:

"like me" "me going" "John he" "can I" "them taking"

"except the offer" "further to NY" "him going" "like us"

"you calling us" "have got" "by us coming" "wish it was over" "where is he at" "John and myself" "whether or not"

ALL OF US NEED TO WORK HARDER TO GET EVERYONE TO SPEAK ENGLISH CORRECTLY, FLUENTLY, AND WITHOUT AN ACCENT.

CHAPTER XIII
"CURRICULA"

Many of our public schools are still living in a nineteenth century academic world. Public schools must provide training to students so they can go to college, or to the job market when they graduate from high school. If the schools are going to do this, they must change the curricula by incorporating technical/trade channels for students who do not intend to go to college.

Changes in the academic channel are also necessary. For example, in English courses we don't need to write poetry, or essays on theoretical subjects. Instead, we need to teach how to write reports, memoranda, etc., like the students will write when they get out of high school and college and into the real world. Also, grammar must be stressed. If you doubt this, listen to people on TV who should be able to speak standard English, but don't.

CREATING TECHNICAL/TRADE CHANNELS IS A MUST FOR ALL SCHOOL DISTRICTS. HOWEVER, THIS WILL BE ONE OF THE HARDEST CHANGES TO MAKE, BECAUSE IT WILL COST MONEY FOR BUILDINGS AND EQUIPMENT.

CHAPTER XIV
"TEACHERS AND ADMINISTRATORS"

In this chapter we stressed the need for reform in the curricula in "teacher colleges." We also advocated the need for change in the selection criteria for principals, superintendents and other education personnel. The criteria we suggested was that the best qualified be selected for the job - not the one who had the required college courses.

Both changes will be a "hard sell" because colleges, education agencies, and administrators are steeped in tradition, and they want to continue as they are.

GOVERNORS, THE BALL IS IN YOUR COURT AGAIN. IF YOU WANT TO MAKE YOUR SCHOOLS

BETTER, YOU MUST SELECT PRINCIPALS, ETC., BASED ON THEIR ABILITY TO CONTROL AND TEACH STUDENTS - NOT ON COURSES TAKEN.

CHAPTER XV
"COLLEGES"

In this chapter we advocated dropping many of the arts courses such as law, psychology, and philosophy, (Humanities), and incorporating more technical courses. We also advocated raising college entrance standards in order to be able to teach college level - not remedial-level courses.

Also, we advocated changes in "teacher colleges." The changes we recommended were to require future teachers to be able to teach two subjects - one of the subjects being science or math. The other change which was recommended was that colleges teach value training to teacher trainees: how to be mother, father, counselor, and confident to their future students.

WE MUST STRENGTHEN TEACHER TRAINING , AND TECHNICAL TRAINING. WE CAN'T AFFORD THE LUXURY OF TRAINING STUDENTS WHO WANT TO STUDY SUBJECTS WHICH DO NOT HAVE AN APPLICATION IN THE REAL WORLD.

AFTERWORD

The authors would like to be optimistic about the future of our schools, but they cannot be for the following reasons:

1. Educators who operate our schools today are the ones who lost control of the schools beginning in 1963, and are the ones who do not know how to regain control. If our educators can't gain control, who can? This sounds drastic, but we need to turn our schools over to business organizations who will operate them as a business. Many of our large businesses operate their own schools now, and are very capable of operating our public schools. One good example is the Ford Motor Company Apprentice Training Program, and there are many other companies who could do a better job than our educators are doing. We would need to give them the authority to make whatever changes they deemed necessary including hiring and firing teachers and administrators. While the businesses are operating our schools, we could train a new cadre of educators who could take over the operation of our schools after the businesses get our schools back on track.

2. Why are such drastic actions necessary such as turning the schools over to businesses? Such actions are necessary, because we do not have time to try to reform our present day educators, and then let them try to reform our schools. We don't have time, because the world is leaving us behind. Other

industrialized countries have education programs now which will train their population to be able to compete in the new and industrialized world.

3. Our problems are compounded by the fact that our minority population is growing faster than we can educate them. If we don't find an immediate solution for minorities, about 25% of our population, by mid-century, will be uneducated and on relief. In order to solve this problem, we must get the minorities out of the ghettos and barrios and into schools where we can teach them to be productive citizens. If we don't solve this problem, we cannot educate everyone, and educate everyone, we must.

The authors can't be optimistic because they know that our educators will not take the bull by the horns and make the changes immediately which have been recommended, even if they were qualified to do so. The politicians will not become a driving force to help improve our education system, because they are too busy making re-election plans, and would probably not be re-elected if they turned the schools over to businesses. They are not looking ahead to see where our country is going. Most of them do not recognize that the poor condition of our schools is an enemy which we must defeat. How do we wake them up? Let's all try writing to them and give them the facts concerning education reform.

As was stated in the FORWARD and PREFACE, we have an enemy who can do more damage than an atomic bomb, and who is already on our shores.

That enemy is the poor condition of our public schools. If we don't fight this enemy, our country will continue it's slide to where it will eventually be a third rate nation, and many of our citizens will be uneducated and hungry.

Why will it continue to go down hill? It will because we don't have a leader who will lead the fight. Why don't we have a leader who will lead the fight? We don't because the U.S. Department of Education doesn't have the authority to lead. All that Department can do is suggest. The authority of the Department of Education should be expanded to include the preparation of standards, course outlines, and syllabi to be used as models for the states to base their changes on. Let's all write to our Congressmen and Senators and ask them to amend the Goals 2000 Act to give the U.S. Department of Education this authority.

The states have the authority and right to educate their own. If we were in a shooting war, the Regular Army and other military services would call in the National Guard and the Reserves, and begin training them to become ready to enter the battle. In the war on education reform, we don't have a Regular Army of Educators who are trained to fight education reform wars. What we do have are fifty state agencies who are operating independently of each other.

A good analogy is that, if we were in a shooting war, we would let each state National Guard march off to fight the war with no direction from a central command. Do you think we would win that war? Another analogy which we have used before is the one of fifty logs floating down a river which leads to the sea. These logs are covered with ants running around in all directions, and each one thinks it is steering. The ants are the state education agencies, educators, school administrators, and school boards from each of the states. We can't continue to let each state fight the war alone. We need a central command who will keep the logs from going out to sea. We won't get a central command who has authority to order changes, because each state is responsible for it's own education program. Therefore, the authors are not optimistic that changes will be made in a reasonable time frame. We hope that the annual reports which will be prepared by the U.S. Department of Education will be a help in improving education in all the states.

Another reason for being pessimistic is that the poor are getting poorer. We must educate everyone, but how to educate the poor seems to be a problem which doesn't have a solution. We could do a better job than we are doing now, if we could afford to take the bright minority students out of their environment, and put them in boarding schools. We can't do this because of the huge national debt we are saddled with. Maybe we could afford this plan by taking bright students, and have them live in barracks which are being made surplus by military draw-down on army posts. Maybe with state and local funds for the education of each student, we might be able to hire teachers and feed the students. We must find a way to educate the poor.

Many of the poor are also the ones who are not motivated to learn. We can't change human nature, but we must find a way to motivate them. Separate Technical/Trade channels will help, because some students will see a reason for going to school. Better training for teachers will also help. An iron-clad law requiring school attendance until eighteen, or until graduated will also help. Such a law will get children off the streets, and into the classroom where the teachers will have the opportunity to motivate and teach them to be good citizens, and to train them to get jobs when they graduate.

It is hard to be optimistic about winning the education reform war as long as our justice system fails to punish law breakers with justifiable punishment. Students know they can get away with almost any crime they commit, and can get away with any misconduct by them in classrooms. Until we get law and order in our classrooms, we cannot win the education reform war.

Our failure to keep up with technical training as more knowledge becomes available is another problem which does not have a plan for solution. It's difficult to see that this will be done, because we are not even teaching what has been available, and there is no concrete plan to turn out all high school graduates who can perform in all academic subjects at the high school level.

The authors are particularly concerned about

educating our minorities, because little or no attention or action is being taken to educate all minorities. Educating all of our minorities should be our number one priority. It is understood that many problems are involved in educating this group, but all of them have solutions except poverty, and no one has found a solution to this problem. Therefore, the authors close the subject by being pessimistic about educating all of our minorities. We hope someone will come up with a solution.

One education subject which has not been addressed is what percentage of our population has the IQ which will be necessary to train them for the high tech jobs which we will have in the future. Any time we mention IQ, a debate is started. On second thought it doesn't open up a debate, it opens up a shouting match. Let's face it - there are many jobs today for which many of our citizens do not have the IQ to be trained. There will be many jobs in the future which will require an even higher IQ than is required for many of today's jobs. We need to be thinking about this fact as we make changes to our education system. The authors are going to leave this subject to those who are more qualified than they.

If anyone who reads this book has a solution to offer for the education problems we now have, or will have in the future, please send it to the authors who will do everything they can to make the solutions widely known.

THE AUTHORS' FINAL WORDS

CHANGES WHICH ARE NECESSARY FOR SCHOOL IMPROVEMENT WILL NOT COME FROM WITHIN THE SCHOOLS. EVERY PARENT, CITIZEN, AND LAW MAKER MUST EXERT AN EXTERNAL FORCE IN ORDER TO INCORPORATE THE CHANGES.

WE MUST MAKE THE NECESSARY CHANGES IN EDUCATION IMMEDIATELY, AND WE MUST EDUCATE EVERYONE. ALSO, WE MUST MAKE CHANGES IN OUR LAWS AND IN OUR PRISON SYSTEM. WE MUST MAKE PARENTS RESPONSIBLE FOR THE EDUCATION AND CONTROL OF THEIR CHILDREN. WE MUST TEACH VALUES IN OUR HOMES AND IN OUR SCHOOLS. LAST, BUT NOT LEAST, WE MUST REVERSE THE SUPREME COURT'S RULING CONCERNING PRAYER IN CLASSROOMS.

IF WE DO NOT DO ALL OF THESE THINGS, THE ECONOMIC LEVELS OF OUR POPULATION BY MID-CENTURY WILL BE APPROXIMATELY AS FOLLOWS:

5%   WILL LIVE IN LUXURY AND WILL HAVE 95% OF THE WEALTH.

10%   WILL HAVE GOOD JOBS AND WILL BE ABLE TO REALIZE THE AMERICAN DREAM.

50% WILL HAVE A JOB, BUT THEIR PAY WILL BE AT OR NEAR THE POVERTY LEVEL, AND THEY WILL NOT BE ABLE TO REALIZE THE AMERICAN DREAM.

35% WILL BE IN PRISON OR ON RELIEF.

DO WE WANT TO FALL TO THE ECONOMIC LEVEL OF THIRD WORLD COUNTRIES? WE DON'T HAVE TO, BUT WE DO HAVE TO EDUCATE EVERYONE, IF WE DON'T WANT THIS TO HAPPEN TO OUR COUNTRY.

ABOUT THE AUTHORS

RODDY SCHNITZ is a Naval Aviator who has many thousands of flight hours in all types of naval aircraft including jet fighters. He retired as the Production Manager for new aircraft and airborne missiles for the Navy. His experience in education has been in the technical field. In this field he served as classroom instructor; branch head; grades, grading, and statistics supervisor; chief of curricula; and principal of a technical school which at one time had an enrolment of over 30,000 students. When the enrolment exceeded the capacity of the school, he contracted with colleges and other technical schools to train some of the students. During the time he was chief of curricula, he supervised the writing of all course materials including texts, text materials, course outlines, syllabi, work projects, and instructor guides. His teaching and industry experience make him well qualified to offer changes needed to improve public education.

KELLY COLE has over twenty years experience in public education. She has taught all grades from primary through high school and adult education. Her experience has been mainly with at-risk students. This teaching experience has given her an insight into the problems involved in educating the poor and the minorities. In order to cope with the problems of teaching these groups of students she developed value training and innovative teaching methods. She also has developed and written curricula for different levels of teaching including workshops for teachers. She has completed extensive post-graduate work above her graduate degree not only in education, but in numerous other disciplines.